Mompreneur

Memoirs

Lisa Kuntze
and 11 Inspiring Co-Authors

Published by Prominence Publishing
www. Prominencepublishing.com

ISBN: 978-1-988925-68-4

Contents

Note to the Reader

Dear reader, if you are an aspiring Mompreneur, we want you to know that you are not alone. We are cheering you on and no matter how hard the journey becomes or how long it may take, we want you to know that it is worth it! This book is dedicated to the courageous co-authors who are generously sharing their inspiring stories of overcoming adversity while somehow managing motherhood and entrepreneurship successfully.

Lisa Kuntze, a Mompreneur of 2 boys and multiple businesses, has brought these women together to uplift and inspire aspiring Mompreneurs. Lisa hosts the Mompreneur Mentor YouTube channel and hopes to create a Mompreneur community that can not only be a supportive group, but also a platform to spotlight Mompreneurs! This book is the first of a series of Memoirs that shed light on amazing Mompreneur stories. When Lisa thought of creating Mompreneur Memoirs she envisioned it as a "chicken soup for the soul" for Mompreneurs. Mothers who are entrepreneurs are often overshadowed by their male counterparts in entrepreneurial media and/or the fact that they balance work and family life is disregarded. Statistically speaking, Mompreneurs usually balance a heavier workload; this inequality in the home needs to be addressed.

So let us share our stories!

Entrepreneurship and motherhood are labor intensive and can be terribly scary and isolating - but your goals are not impossible - regardless of the adversities and complexities you must face and overcome to reach them. We are here to share our stories with you and spotlight strong female figures who are paving the way and blazing the trail so you know that you can too!

If you're a Mompreneur with an amazing story who would like to participate in this series, please join us for the next publication. We would love to hear from you.

Lisa Kuntze

CHAPTER ONE

Moving On After a Con

By Lisa Kuntze

Hello, my name is Lisa, and I'm an ECommerce Mompreneur. I have built and sold three ECommerce brands. I became a mom when I was 24 and had a second son when I was 28. As soon as I had my first son, I knew I wanted to be home with him. Unfortunately, being home with your kids doesn't pay the bills. I needed to find a way to make money from home. I believe that mothers make great entrepreneurs because we are used to wearing so many hats. We are used to juggling many different things, and a business requires you to juggle. I started nannying in my home as my first entrepreneurial gig. This allowed me to make money while watching my son. Next, I started a digital agency while studying towards my bachelor's degree, which I eventually achieved. I managed social media for local businesses at an affordable monthly retainer. This allowed me to save up some funds and launch my first ECommerce brand, Mindful Bohemian. I decided I would risk the money I was putting into it and have zero expectations of success. I spent many nights working on my ECommerce store, getting it set up and teaching myself to run the business. The first month I made 5k in sales. I doubled it the second month and tripled it the third. We had a six figure first year and scaled quickly. It was very successful for me. I enjoyed it and wanted to add to my ECommerce portfolio. The margins in fashion are low, so I decided I would start dropshipping high-ticket products with higher profit margins. I launched two high-ticket ECommerce shops that did very well. My success afforded us to go on vacations, purchase our first home, and plan our wedding! I never felt more rewarded than I did funding vacations and smiles for my family. Of course, I could not have done it without the support of my husband; we're a team.

It is extremely fulfilling to know you are able to make money while being a mom, and if you are able to do it, you should be proud! It is a constant balancing act and takes a lot of patience. Mompreneurs have it twice as hard as entrepreneurs. This is especially true when you are still the maid, the driver, the nanny, the teacher, the chef, the laundress, etc. Now you also get to be the accountant, marketer, I.T. person, social media manager, brand specialist, customer satisfaction specialist, web developer, business strategist, team leader, company cheerleader and much more. It wasn't easy. I worked while my family slept. I struggled with bookkeeping, finding trustworthy employees overseas to scale, and running three businesses. Still, I made it happen. I learned so much from my business. I have so many skill sets and talents because of my business. Things were working well in Ecommerce. It is and was booming! Knowledge is power, so I learned everything I could about ECommerce. The driving factor behind these businesses was simply to bring more income to my family. My family was and always will be my "why".

That is why I felt like I had failed them terribly when I was scammed online; the guilt and shame was overwhelming.

I had attempted to scale to the next level and needed to outsource or grow my team in order to do so. Here I am minding my own business, working hard and growing and along comes a psychopath. I cannot believe I did not see it. This scam artist preyed on people in a large Facebook group called "Clickfunnels". I sent him cash from our liquid savings to complete work—work which he never completed. I called him out in the group and reported him, but he coerced me into taking the first post down. He told me if I took it down, he would do the work I paid for. I told him I required a refund and could no longer work with him. He refused and would go silent. He told others in the group I was lying and that I had made everything up. He publicly bullied me on their Facebook page. He played a mean game of psychological warfare. He victimized me with no conscience or care for the harm he had caused to me, my business, my family, my children, and our finances. I realized he would never do the work, and I posted in the group again to warn people. When I did this, many other victims came forward. We all proceeded to file complaints with the FBI for fraud. We wrote complaints online with the BBB and did everything we could to speak out against this scam artist.

It is unfortunate that criminals like this are not pursued to a greater extent. I was so disgusted with the criminal justice system. They did little to nothing to be of assistance. The FBI didn't get back to us, even though the group neared 20 victims and a substantial amount of stolen money. This man, who was going by the name of Jeremy Derks, changed his name and continued to scam and con people. The admins of the group eventually banned him, but he has made other accounts and continues to prey on people.

I ended up suing him in court, I was self-represented and confident as I had successfully represented myself previously. I won in court because he never showed up and was obviously a scam artist. As a con artist, who lived across the country, he would bounce around and make it nearly impossible for me to collect the judgment against him. I tried to levy his bank account, but he had closed the account. He had stolen our money and gotten away with it. I didn't have the bandwidth to continue to pursue him and the negative energy was weighing down on me. I decided to stop pursuing it and let karma have a turn. I still don't know what became of the con artist. Maybe in the future I will have justice, the judgment is good until paid, but I am not getting my hopes up.

This was a valuable lesson for me. It was so hard for me to come to terms with. I could never imagine doing this to anyone or anyone doing it to me. I trusted this person and he victimized me and took advantage of me. The scam had led me to neglect my businesses, and the stress was hard on my family and my health. It really affected me; I was also caring for my Mother post-stroke and simply could not manage everything. I was melancholy for weeks. It gave me PTSD in business and made it hard for me to trust networking or meeting people online to work with. Shortly after the scam, I sold my three websites and felt like quitting entrepreneurship. It felt like all people were bad people. I felt as if I could not trust anyone or rely on anyone. It was a painful lesson to learn. I did end up making more friends online and engaging with the entrepreneurial community, even with PTSD and anxiety making it difficult.

Many people from the Clickfunnels community reached out and offered services for free to help me get the job I paid for done, but none of them panned out. It just wasn't working. Things were not working, and I took it as a sign that it was time to toss in my entrepreneurial towel. I took time to recover myself and find new purpose. I started exercising, went on a vacation, did everything I could to overcome the situation. I decided it was better to move on.

It is so important to overcome adversity. It is the most important thing we must do in life. No life will be free of adversity. I feel this scam made me a stronger person in many ways, but I would not wish it on anyone. It helped me learn that I need to have more grit, be tougher and more business savvy. It made me stronger for my family, my friends and mostly for myself. My ability to overcome a victimizing situation and switch my mindset from the victim to the victor is a triumph in my eyes. I needed to take my power back from this person, and by telling my story, I am doing so. I have stopped blaming myself for this person's actions. It isn't my fault. It is never the victim's fault. I learned to stick up for myself with the lawsuit. I did stick up for myself. I did win. I did get back on the horse and refused to let this one person take my power away.

I have since launched MommEComm and I am now teaching other mothers how to build ECommerce businesses. I have started a YouTube Channel, "Mompreneur Mentor", and launched this first book for the Mompreneur Memoirs series. I have also decided I am going to work on an invention I have patented. To help me start off, I joined the Founder Institute, a global business accelerator program. The program introduced me to amazing entrepreneurs like myself and inspired me. It helped me feel better about entrepreneurship again. It opened my eyes to possibilities I had not dreamed of before. I completed the rigorous program in the spring of 2020, during the pandemic. As I write this we are in quarantine and although I am unsure what the future holds, I am excited about it again.

About the Author

Lisa Kuntze has always been a creative. She enjoys creating art, music and growing ideas into businesses. Lisa's desire to work from home, travel and be available to her family led her into Entrepreneurship. Lisa is a self taught Mompreneur (@MompreneurMentor) who started in digital marketing and grew into ECommerce. Lisa has a voice to give under- served Mompreneurs hope, help them cope and a business model to reach success! She hosts a Mompreneur Mentor YouTube Vlog, created the Mompreneur Memoirs series and offers her digital course, MommEComm, for those who want to learn the step- by-step route to high-ticket dropshipping success! It covers tech, legal, marketing, products, niche, scaling and more!

CHAPTER TWO

How to Pivot When the Going Gets Tough

By TaVia Iles

You can guarantee that life will find a way to humble you. Count on it, expect it, and honestly, just prepare for it! As I type these words, the little voice in my head is screaming this is so easy to say but difficult to implement. Notice I said, "difficult" to implement, not impossible.

My goal is to encourage you to do the difficult, and that is to PIVOT when you are faced with obstacles, challenges and even trauma. There is a chance you are probably thinking, "Okay, lady. Who are you to tell me to PIVOT when I've experienced the most difficult thing in my life?!" Just wait. I'm going to share my story with you as well as the journey it took to get my life back on track and move forward. Here is the short summary, one day at a time! Okay, seriously. I have more to give you!

Let's start with, "Who is TaVia?"

I asked the random question to those around me, "What are three words that describe me?" In return, I heard words such as strong, independent, courageous, fighter, intelligent, beautiful, bold, and this list goes on. I'm a Capricorn, and we are known for our stubbornness, ambition, and drive. I believe every person should have equal rights. Every person should have medical insurance and quality education. I believe that, if everyone was able to start on a level playing field, their potential to be great and do great is endless. I believe that no matter how smart and driven you are, you have to have a belief in a Higher Power, and you may call it whatever you like. I believe that.

While the American philosophy is to be independent, we must become a community of one, for this is the only way we will truly be able to survive in times of chaos, recessions, depressions, and sickness. I believe that faith is the substance of things hoped for and the evidence of things unseen. I believe love will go a long way, but love alone is not always enough.

I am a child of circumstances that I hear so many speak about, circumstances that have kept many people from reaching their potential: poor, from a single parent home, the head of a single parent home, a minority, divorced, a woman, a disabled person. I fit into all these categories, yet I have tried diligently to not let them define me! I believe one of the greatest influences in my life has been my older brother who currently lives with me. He is 30 years old, has Autism, and was born with brain damage, which has left him developmentally delayed. The doctors never had an explanation as to why he was dealt this hand, and despite popular belief, my mother did not drink or smoke and was not physically abused during her pregnancy. I learned very early that my brother was special. I always like to use the word special because it meant he stood out from the rest. He was above ordinary and beyond normal! From my brother, I learned what compassion actually means, to love unconditionally when it may never be returned and doesn't make sense. From my childhood experiences with my brother, I understood what Jesus meant when he walked with society's "undesirables". From my humble upbringing, I realized the world was not fair, but that it could be one day. If I just worked hard enough and fought diligently, I, my brother, and others like me would prevail.

God created me as a fighter. Some may say I'm aggressive, others called me insubordinate, but I always knew my purpose here on Earth was to speak for those who had no voice, those who felt helpless, and for those who may have lost their way. I wear my battlefield armor daily because those who continued to make the world unjust never took days off. I stay ready, always in preparation mode, because no sooner than one victory is achieved there will be another which needs to be forged.

The purpose I believed was created for me has been challenged and wounded critically. We, as people, will always be challenged. They say God doesn't give you anything you can't handle, but to every person who wants to tell me that, ask yourself if you could handle planning and carrying out your own child's funeral. Ask yourself if you can continue to have compassion for people when people continue to disregard your feelings! Can you continue to fight when no one fought for your child's life? Will you continue to respect the current health insurance system, the very system that denied your child the medical treatment to give him a fighting chance to have a future?

What would you do if you had a disability which could end your life one day? You can't tell anyone because people will pass judgment upon you. How would you feel knowing your medical insurance only takes cares of this disability minimally? Better yet, how would you feel if your child had this disability, and your resources were limited? I have a disability. Based upon my disability I am entitled to government services and accommodations in the classroom and work place, but I don't utilize them. To access these services means I have to tell the world "what's wrong with me," and to do that would change the way in which people interacted with and thought of me. For those who think otherwise, until you have a disability, keep your uninformed opinions to yourself!

I present a small part of my personal story because I present this urgent question to you, the reader: "What will it take for you to take action?" How much has to be taken from you before you decide to get in the fight? Will it be the loss of a child? A life-threatening disability? I pray that no one has to endure some of the pain I have endured, but I do ask that you learn from my life experience, and don't waste time getting involved in the fight for justice and equality for all people! Let my story be your story. Let my pain remind you that we still have a long way to go!

All right! Now you know a little bit about me, let's talk about how we move forward. How do we begin again?

We P.I.V.O.T!

Merriam-Webster defines pivot:

Definition of pivot (Entry 1 of 3)

> 1: a shaft or pin on which something turns

> 2 a: a person, thing, or factor having a major or central role, function, or effect

> b: a key player or position

> specifically: an offensive position of a basketball player standing usually with back to the basket to relay passes, shoot, or provide a screen for team-mates

> 3: the action of pivoting

> especially: the action in basketball of stepping with one foot while keeping the other foot at its point of contact with the floor.

Let's focus on the third definition "3: the action of pivoting, especially: the action in basketball of stepping with one foot while keeping the other foot at its point of contact with the floor."

Keeping one foot as a point of contact basically means that this foot is planted firmly in the ground allowing the basketball player to move around with his other foot and body in order to find the best direction to move forward without losing his current footing. Once the player has identified the direction he wants to move in, he can then take his free foot and put that foot in front of the other in the direction he wants to go. One more point to make: When he moves in a direction he has deemed has the least resistance overall strategically, this gets him close to scoring the point, etc.

Yes, my friend. I am asking you to PIVOT and more with one foot in front of the other. I will share with you what that looks like.

P: Plan and Prepare—When it's time to move forward, one foot in front of the other, you must plan on what you want your end result to look like. In the planning process, you begin to work out the vision of what moving forward looks like for you. Make sure you dream big and then think of what that will do for you. When planning, make sure it is realistic and obtainable and that, overall, you are indeed moving in a direction that works best for you. Make sure you decide on a start date. You don't need to wait for a Monday, a new month, or a new year. You can start in the next hour or next day. Just get into action.

In the preparation stage, you will begin to gather all the resources to implement that plan. Does the plan require changing your schedule? Do that. Does it require asking for help via accountability? Find someone and enroll them in your goal of moving forward. Think through this list. Exhaust the brainstorming stage that will support your ability to put your plan into action. A plan we fail to prepare for will do nothing for us. Plan and Prepare to start!

I: Implement and Initiate Tracking—Implement! Remember that plan? Now you must put it into motion based on the start date you decided upon in the first step. Once the plan is implemented, you must initiate a way to track your progress.

A tracked outcome grows or is achieved. Based on what your desired outcome is, you must identify key factors which let you know you are making progress. If we use a fitness plan (healthy living) as an example, then tracking may involve monitoring how many times you work out in a week or month, food consumption, drinking water, and sleep. If the desired outcome is better mental health/wellbeing, how many times you attend therapy, practice meditation, etc. can be tracked. This simple act of tracking will help you assess if you are making progress or if you are not.

Side note: If you see you are not making progress, remember the accountability partner from the P stage? This would be a great time to check in with them and share your tracking sheet to receive support and encouragement to get back on track. If you are making progress, smile, do a little dance, write a little note to yourself to remember that feeling. If you see you are not making progress, then begin again, in the next minute, the next hour, or the next day. No grand date makes a plan happen, just doing it does.

V: Visualize the Victory—I encourage you to focus and visualize what the end goal will look like. Will you be healthier? Will that be a new job? Will that be a happier relationship? Will that be consistent self-care and love? Whatever the desired outcome is, visualize it every day for a few moments. Write it down, and talk about it as if it has already happened. See yourself happy. Visualize the positive effects on you and those around you. This is such an important step. If we don't begin to see ourselves in a new position, a new mindset, then we will not achieve it.

Start small if you must, by having a single statement of how you will feel when you have achieved the desired outcome. Then, grow from there.

O: Optimize every Opportunity—No matter how small or big, you make it count. See every option as an opportunity to grow, develop, and become better. Know that even setbacks are opportunities to maximize. When presented with an option or opportunity, take the time to brainstorm how the outcome can be beneficial to you. Document this by journaling your thoughts regarding the opportunity. Don't keep everything in your head. Get the thoughts out and evaluate those potential outcomes.

T: Trust the Process and Transform—Hey sis!! Here is a very important part I want you to focus on. You have to Trust the process of growth, moving forward, accountability, vitalizing the victory opportunities, and allow for the process to refine you so that you can transform into a better version of yourself or a better situation for you.

There will be times when it will feel weird, that nothing is happening, or that you are a fool for even thinking you can do something different. HOWEVER, I promise you if you allow the process to work, you will transform, and when you do, it will be an amazing experience.

Here are a few tips I want you to be aware of during the transformational process.

1. Set no time on when you should be transformed. What you are going through will determine what is an acceptable time. As I shared, I have lost a child, and grief is hard and reoccurring. There is no end date for grief, but I know that, and I allow my grief to occur and work through those feelings when they happen. I don't beat myself up. I just know this is the journey I am on. Each time it occurs, it doesn't last as long, and I am able to rebound sooner.

2. There is a chance that you will change, and people will notice and comment. Sometimes those comments are not positive, but ignore them! Everyone in your life now will not be there when you have transformed, and that's okay. Visualize the victory and the better version of yourself.

3. Be open to refining your plan. You may not get it right the first time, and that's okay. Maybe you'll find out you want a different outcome, and that's okay, too. You are unique and human, and we change often. Journal it, evaluate the outcomes, and optimize every opportunity.

4. Affirm yourself daily! Find a mantra, a scripture or a word which tells you every day that you will make it, you will be successful, you are enough!! Sometimes you will need to affirm yourself a million times in a day! Do that!! Do what is needed to keep you uplifted.

No matter where you are starting or what you have gone through, I truly believe we have the ability to PIVOT and design a new outcome for ourselves. Focus on that, and put your energy into a new you. Okay, Sis! I believe in you! You got this!

About the Author

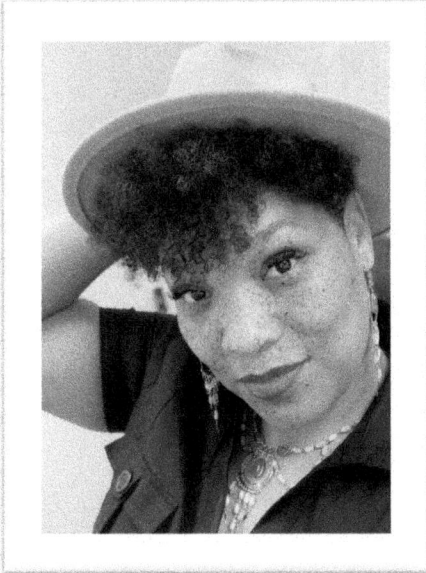

TaVia Iles loves all things that empower women to be their best self. Her professional background consist of being a social worker of 20 years and now she owns a communications business where she helps small business owners and women solopreneurs have the audacity to be seen. She uses her experience to empower women to use their stories to connect with their audience and convert to profitable business. When she isn't working you can find her homeschooling her 3 youngest children along with her husband and visiting their adult son at college. To learn more about TaVia connect with her on IG and Facebook under TaVia Iles communications and her personal IG @Thecommunicationschic or tavia@taviailes.com

CHAPTER THREE

My Entrepreneurial Journey and Five Lessons Learned

By Anita Rajendra

Ever doubt yourself? Ever feel the "Imposter Syndrome"? Question yourself and what you're doing? I have. Although I have founded two companies, I still feel it.

My first company, La Belle Bump, is what started me on my entrepreneurial journey. I founded La Belle Bump, which is a company that rents maternity and nursing clothes to help women feel and look confident and beautiful during their pregnancies. The second company, Mina & Vine, was born out of insights gained from La Belle Bump. The Mina & Vine scarf is a first of its kind, a patent pending, smart scarf. Functionally, it can be worn as a nursing cover or as a scarf at any time in a woman's life. It can be worn 10+ different ways, from poncho to sash to vest. We also use magnetic fasteners and temperature-regulated fabric. Both companies were created to help solve problems women face. Who wants to buy a whole new wardrobe while pregnant? After all, you may only wear the items a few times, but have to spend a small fortune for quality clothes! And as a new mom, you have a lot of things to buy for your baby. Why add another disposable item by buying a nursing cover that will be useless after you're done nursing? On average, each American throws away roughly 81 pounds of clothing every year. So I made a conscious effort with both companies to help reduce waste and increase the longevity of clothing items. That is an important aspect of both these companies.

Avoiding waste is something that I probably inherited from my immigrant parents. As immigrants, my parents were both frugal and hyper-focused on education. I went through the "normal route" of a child of an immigrant. I studied hard, focused on school, got into a good college, and went on to graduate school.

Following this, I went into a career in marketing at top Fortune 500 Companies. My first job after earning an MBA was at Saturn, a General Motors brand. I moved to Detroit, nervous but excited to officially start my career. And I loved it! Saturn was a great place for a marketer. It was a customer-focused company. I loved that we, as professionals, were supposed to look for and create "wow" moments for customers. I remember in particular one promotion that I was leading - Sponsorship of The Moscow Ballet's 'Great Russian Nutcracker'. Part of the sponsorship included a car giveaway. When the winner was announced, we found out that the winner was a nursing student who was driving a damaged, old car. She really needed and deserved a new car so we decided to go the extra mile. We sent an official poster of The Nutcracker and everyone that "touched" this specific car in the factory signed it. The day the winner was going to get the car, we arranged for a limo to pick her and her parents up and take them to a nice dinner before arriving at the Saturn dealership to pick up her new car. The car was wrapped in a bow, had balloons around it and everyone at the dealership cheered her on as she came into the store. We were able to make this "small" moment so much more memorable for the winner. Creating these "surprise & delight" moments has become something integral in my companies.

After working at Saturn and living in Detroit for several years, my husband and I decided to make a change and move. Atlanta, GA, was where we ended up. I started networking while still in Detroit, trying to make connections so I could find a job in Atlanta. That proved to be successful and soon I had landed a job with The Coca-Cola Company. A marketer's dream. I was able to work on high profile brands and projects, and launch new brands and programs. I remember when I started at The Coca-Cola Company, I thought I would be there 3, maybe 5 years. I wanted to work for a smaller company because eventually I wanted to start my own company. What that was I didn't know, but the idea of starting something from scratch was exciting and invigorating to me. Although I had no idea how to start a business. Well, two years into my time at The Coca-Cola Company, I found out I was pregnant. I had always wanted a family and to become a mom. But was this the right time? Of course, I've since realized that there's no "right time". No "perfect" time. And so this became our time. I worked through my first pregnancy, went on maternity leave and went back afterwards. I knew something had to change because honestly I didn't have a work/life balance (does it exist?) and no idea how to gain any balance. My solution? Job sharing. It seemed like a great idea. I could share the job I enjoyed with someone else. I continued working through 2 more pregnancies. So, the original 3-5 years was turning into more than that.

After 8 years, I was gaining less enjoyment from my work. I was ready for a change. I was burned out. I was going through the motions. I also wasn't really excited about other job opportunities. I had more than toyed with my own business ideas a couple of times in the past. I had seriously looked into potential franchise operations, and looked at creating a clothing swap platform. Nothing had ever progressed far; however, I knew that eventually, I wanted to start a business. "Some day." That was my goal. Whenever people would ask me what my dream job was, I would respond "owning my own business". But it was abstract. There was no plan. It was something I had said for literally years. And I was continuing to say that. I was ready for a change, to do something else. It seemed like the perfect opportunity but I was nervous. First of all, I didn't know what type of business. What if I failed? What if I didn't like it? What if I didn't make money?

I was struggling, and not happy. I didn't know what to do. Eventually, I threw my hands up. And I made the decision that I had to either stop talking about wanting to start a company or take action. I decided to take action. Once that decision was made, I gained so much clarity. I felt relief. I had a plan, or at least a direction. I was able to start moving. I started to develop the next steps. I gave myself 6 months to "figure things out" and I was going to leave my corporate job. No matter what. I knew realistically I could not work in a demanding corporate job, raise 3 children, and start a business. Something had to give. So, the corporate job would give.

I was methodical about my plans. Maybe too much, but it helped me. I'm a planner and I wanted to take some of the risk out - or at least it made me feel like I was taking some of the risk out. During the 6 months I had given myself, I started to see what local resources there were. I networked and talked to other entrepreneurs. I started brainstorming business ideas. I started with my life and problems I saw. What solutions could I apply? Would people be interested in this solution? Would they pay for it? What would the potential startup cost be? Were there other companies doing this? I had a list of questions that I would answer for each idea. Ideas came from everywhere. In fact, the idea for La Belle Bump came while in a meeting in my corporate job. I remember that before the meeting started, everyone was chit-chatting, and a colleague who was pregnant was complaining about buying maternity clothes. She didn't want to spend the money on something she wouldn't need longer term. Since I was in a brainstorming mode, that conversation started my creative juices flowing and I thought there had to be a better way. So that started me on a path - what was the better way?

I eventually had a short list of potential ideas. Real ideas. I then narrowed down the list and focused on where my passion was. After all, if I was going to be doing this fulltime, I had to be interested in it and want to do it. I focused on my "why". Once the list was narrowed down, I got feedback from other entrepreneurs and potential customers. All this work led me to what eventually became La Belle Bump.

My "why" for La Belle Bump was, and continues to be, wanting to help women. I personally believe that pregnancy is an amazing time in a woman's life and should be celebrated. But so many times we don't feel like ourselves, our body is constantly changing, and we may be physically sick so we don't appreciate that time. I wanted to create something that would help women feel and look confident and beautiful during their pregnancy.

It wasn't easy. I had made the decision about what the company was, but what was next? This was not my field of expertise. I had never worked in retail or fashion. It would have been nice to have a step by step checklist or someone to give me pointers. But I didn't have those things and so I had to figure it out on my own. I probably, actually I know, took a longer route with some things. For example, finding maternity brands that I wanted to carry. I had to do the research and try to get a contact. I eventually found out that most brands have sales rep and once I found one, he/she could help introduce me to other brands and other sales reps. The fear and doubt still existed. And at times it could be overwhelming. What really was I doing? I had to invest capital for the clothes to start with. But at the same time, I didn't want to spend much. I was very tight to the vest when it came to spending. After all, it was my money and not corporate money that I was investing now. And honestly, I had no idea if this would even work, and even if it did work; when would I recoup my investment?

Starting this company also impacted my personal life. We cut back on some things. No more nanny, for one thing. I had to try and work while caring for children. I also had to incorporate my husband more into my work. I hadn't really done this while in the corporate world. We were in different industries and didn't get intimately involved in each other's work. But now I was using our personal money, time and space to fund this new company without having the background, knowledge, or a crystal ball to know if it would succeed.

I remember launching the company. The website went live and I announced it on my personal Facebook page. I was so excited. I was ready for orders to come pouring in. But, crickets. Nothing! No orders. Immediately I got worried. Was it not a good idea? Too expensive? Was my research all wrong? But I had to pause and step back. I realized I was telling my circle about it. Although I was getting a lot of positive feedback, they were not my target market. Most of them were done with pregnancies. After all, I was. This notion of "if I build it they will come" was not realistic. I had to market. So I started from the grassroots. I went to OB offices to see if they would hand out flyers to their new pregnancy patients. It started slow, but word of mouth was what really helped sell the company in those early days. I remember my first big break was when a customer posted about our company in an online group. From that one post, we nearly doubled our number of customers! Word of mouth was and continues to be a big driver for us.

I've learned so much throughout this journey of entrepreneurship. Both companies are still in early yet different stages, so there's definitely lots of room for further improvement and growth. And yes; I still feel the doubt at times. But I also try to remember, appreciate and celebrate the accomplishments. A few specific lessons that have been ingrained in me are:

1. Stop talking and start doing. As I mentioned earlier, this was the catalyst for my journey into the startup world. But it's something that I have to continue to remind myself. Instead of over analyzing something and mulling for days over it, you need to take action and move forward.

2. "Done is better than perfect." This is something I struggled with. I can be a perfectionist, especially coming from the corporate client world. I wanted things "just right". But when starting a new business, it's important to get your product or service in front of real customers to see if it resonates with them. Something you may have spent a lot of time on to perfect may not be what they care about.

3. Network. Network. Network. I can't tell you how many times I learned something from a

networking event or coffee meeting that saved me money or time. In fact, I learned about the web platform I launched La Belle Bump on during a coffee with someone I met at a conference. It saved me time and thousands of dollars.

4.   Take time for yourself. Starting a business can be lonely and overwhelming. It's important to recharge. There are many times where I have to walk away from work and take a few hours off and do something for me that is not related to work.

5.   Confidence is key. You have to sell your product and yourself. You can do it. You have the ability and capability; believe in yourself. Forget the imposter syndrome.

About the Author

Anita Rajendra is a Founder & CEO. She started her entrepreneurial journey by launching La Belle Bump, a company that rents stylish, high-quality maternity and nursing clothes. Anita created La Belle Bump to help women feel and look confident and beautiful during their pregnancy by focusing on providing a premium and personal experience without the high price tags.

From learnings leading La Belle Bump, Anita ventured into her second business and co-founded Mina & Vine, a patent pending nursing scarf. The "Smart Scarf" is the first of its kind, using temperature regulated fabric, magnetic fasteners and stylish prints. It can also be worn in more than 10 ways allowing it to easily become a staple in your wardrobe.

Prior to her entrepreneurial pursuits, Anita was a Marketing leader with strong, award-winning consumer marketing experience at The Coca-Cola Company and Saturn, a General Motors brand. During her 13 years at these companies, she led various teams and programs in brand strategy, digital marketing, media planning and promotions.

She currently lives in Atlanta, GA with her husband and 3 children. She enjoys time with family and friends, traveling and trying new restaurants.

Connect with Anita:

La Belle Bump: www.LaBelleBump.com

Mina & Vine: www.MinaAndVine.com

Anita Rajendra: www.LinkedIn.com/in/anitarajendra

CHAPTER FOUR

I Just Wanted a Nice Laundry Room

By Molly Blomeley Hamby

I just wanted a nice laundry room.

I've always been energetic and what most would call unsettled. I thought it was a bad thing for most of my life, but after some soul searching, I've grown to accept my wild spirit. In other words, I like to stay in a movement phase at all times. Sometimes that has worked and other times, not so much. As an adult, I wanted so much more. I wanted the house fixed. I wanted to work and feel a sense of purpose. I wanted to be home with my young girls. I wanted to make elaborate dinners. I wanted to throw fun, adorable birthday parties. I didn't want to be at the parties, though. I wanted to sit and think about things, like flowers, the trees swaying in the wind, and the shapes of the clouds. I wanted to be alone. I wanted to be healthy again. I wanted my auto-immune disease to disappear. I wanted a career. I wanted someone to listen to my feelings and care about what I was actually saying.

I did create most of that. I worked a few hours in the morning (with one baby on my hip) and spent time with both girls in the afternoon. I did what people wanted, and I shied away from stress. Happiness wasn't there. I was doing what everyone else wanted for me. My marriage was based on whatever he "thought" was right. When I energetically voiced my thoughts, he would agree with me and then do the opposite. When I found something I wanted to try or learn, no one else seemed interested.

The Laundry Room

I had been talking about my dream laundry room for 10 years. I designed it with bright colors and vintage eclectic pieces. The one reason I agreed to buy the house he wanted was the laundry room would eventually be perfect. For some reason, my happiness was in a laundry room. I'd never had a real laundry room like the ones with cabinets and things, a space for me.

This house was perfect, complete with a blank laundry room with floor-to-ceiling windows and a door that could be closed. I'd been ready for this since I was 15 and designed a house with my dad. I brought professionals out and got quote after quote. In early August, he promised me my new laundry room by my birthday in late November. I can't explain the excitement. I had received an inheritance and I was going to use $2000 for the perfect room. I waited and waited.

The night before my birthday, he suggested going out shopping and for dinner. "Are the contractors swooping in and hanging the cabinets?" We went to eat and then stopped by our local building store. "Maybe I'm picking out some accessories!" He walked to the cabinet aisle and asked what I wanted, and I just stood there. "I've already given that to you. We agreed to use someone to hang the ones I picked out." I then looked down at my watch and it was 8 pm on the night before he'd promised countless times I would receive the ONE thing I desperately wanted. I knew then that he hadn't planned anything for my birthday and things would never be the same.

For some reason, I assumed this project would be different. I assumed he'd meant what he said. I assumed he knew what meant a lot to me. I assumed he wanted to make me happy. I assumed wrong. I had become very used to things not getting done or vacations not being taken because he'd changed his mind. I now know that he never had intentions in the first place.

I began making my own decisions immediately. I drank wine because I'd always wanted to. I started researching being a single mom. I started looking at making money on my own. I bought a pair of expensive leggings because I had always wanted a pair. I took a full-time job with the company I had worked with for years. He was livid. I was okay, and I kept being okay with every step.

Two horrendous years later, after a custody battle which involved lies, private investigators, restraining orders, numerous therapists, and ALL of my inheritance, I took my girls and drove away. I drove to the only place I could: a hotel. It was awful and eye-opening. I was officially at the bottom. We then began sleeping on my best friend's guest room floor. I lay awake each night crying after the girls fell asleep but tried to seem okay when they were there. When they were gone, I lay there and cried and barely moved until I had to get up for work. I lost 20 pounds in a month. My disease was exerting its dominance and was about to kill me. I didn't care at all. It could do whatever the Hell it wanted at this point.

After months of depression and fear, I finally started realizing that I was the one who would finish this story. It was my story. I stood and began climbing out little by little.

My business story is interesting with many ups and downs, but it's a story I am proud of. I worked for a company which provided wellness services to a Fortune 500 company. The two companies argued constantly, and I was the go-between. One company manager would call me to ask the other company a question and so on. They wouldn't even send each other emails. I started researching each of the jobs and how things were being handled. I called an attorney and discussed every little detail. I found an accountant, and he sat and explained every detail I asked about. I then called the Fortune 500 company's attorney and stated that I would be interested in making a bid when the bid was reopened in four months.

silence

"Wow, Molly. We've never had a single-person company ask that before. I'm not sure what to say." Several days later, he called back and gave me guidelines. I would have to be a company with a legal name, a company with the usual means of liability insurance and so forth, and I would need to have the backing to do it all. I said, "No problem." I hung up and began running as quietly and as quickly as I could. Only three other people knew what I was doing. I developed a business plan, a logo, researched and wrote a bid with their specifications, and began researching employees, etc.

I spent hours on the phone with my dad, a life-long businessman, discussing options and strategies. I had spent every dime I had in the divorce, and I was determined to not borrow money from my family either, but I clearly needed money somehow. I went to a bank and was denied a loan because my business was too young. The only money I had was my daughter's college fund. My daughter would need that money two years later. I fought with that concept for days until I decided I had to. I wrote and rewrote my bid at least 25 times. Each time, my dad scrutinized every word.

The bidding process was sealed until all bids had been accepted. This meant I would surely be fired if my company found out I was their main competitor. I opened a new credit card and prepared myself to not receive a paycheck, and that's exactly what happened. Four months without pay, and I was awarded the contract. I hung the phone up and called my dad immediately. "Oh shit. I'm not sure I really have the courage to do this." His only advice was, "If you go down, at least you tried."

Try is exactly what I did. Every night, after my girls went to bed, I worked. I wrote drafts of programs. I emailed potential employees. I read about every company I could and their wellness programming. I signed up and began furthering my education. I did this all while my daughters slept.

Another six months passed, and I had my grand opening. I was absolutely petrified but I never showed it. Either I would crash and lose everything, or I would succeed. I was proud either way. The ONLY goal I set for myself was to pay my daughter back, and I did within 12 months.

Two years later, I am the woman I thought I was all along: an unsettled, energetic and spirited woman who does whatever I want. What I want is a successful business, to make my own schedule, a happy family, a loving home, and to help others. I have grown my company to 22 employees and opened a second location. I also launched an international fitness business with a partner.

Both girls have a role in the businesses and have blossomed into creative and vibrant women. Even our cat has a part in the business making clients laugh and smile. You can't tell me that I can't buy a $5 item. You can't tell me to clean up my living room. You can't tell me that my hair is too crazy. I make my own decisions now for my house, my life, my body and my career. When I walk in a room, people notice and want to talk to me, not because of what you might imagine, but I believe because I have created this persona, one that is truly me. I still love creating crazy menus and parties, but I love when the guests leave even more. I love finding vintage objects and restoring them or repurposing them into a wild piece which shows more of my personality. I love living completely open and honest.

Guess who is thriving? Everyone around me. My girls are comfortable in their own skins. My employees show up and expect a certain honesty from me. If they mess up, I'm the first one to tell them. If they are doing well, I let them shine. If they are unsure of themselves, I give them the push they need to rise up. I want everyone around me to understand that rising up should always happen. I expect you to want to do better and improve every aspect of your life, and if you call that unsettled or spirited, then that's okay, too.

What's not important to me right now? A damn laundry room! I no longer care that I don't have an awesome and spacious laundry room. My laundry room does have cabinets and the walls are as white as it comes. There's always tons of shit that has fallen behind the washer, and I rarely buy the good laundry detergent.

I'm not even sure what is in the cabinets, and I'm completely okay with that, too.

About the Author

Molly Blomeley Hamby is a 3-time business owner that specializes in all things fitness and nutrition. After facing struggles in life such as an eating disorder, diagnosis of an autoimmune disease and a nasty divorce, she had no choice but to stand and create the life she wanted for herself and her girls. That is exactly what she did. She built multiple businesses while managing her disease and caring for two girls, and reached six-figures within one year! She currently lives in Birmingham, AL with her two girls, Annabelle and Haley Jane, her beloved calico cat Beau and her new husband, Wayne.

Molly works in person for her two facilities in the Birmingham, AL area. She works with online clients from all over the world and loves connecting with clients. She also loves all things vintage, hiking and traveling.

Connect with Molly Blomeley Hamby

IG: molly_blomeley

FB: Molly Blomeley Fitness & Nutrition

CHAPTER FIVE

How I Went From a "Hot Mess Mama" to Success...

By Heather Zeveney

My company, Improve Your Tomorrow Health, LLC, was created in 2018 with the intention of incorporating wellness into the lives of families. As an Advanced Practice Nurse, I saw such a large need to do more to improve the health of patients besides prescribing medication.

It all began with my personal health journey. I needed to share my successful blueprint with others. I was a lifelong point-counting weight watcher and yo-yo dieter, but I had to find something more sustainable. I started by eating cleaner and removing toxins from my home because I was considering starting a family and wanted to keep my animals healthy, too. These simple changes allowed me to conceive easily late in life and maintain a healthy pregnancy and delivery, lose weight, and improve my health in many ways. It also decreased my fiancé's heart disease. His cardiologist was amazed! Plus, my dogs outlived the average life expectancy of their breed.

Since then, my business became a full circle of holistic health and wellness, incorporating preventative measures and getting to the why beneath the why with health and life coaching that uses habit changing techniques and support. My recipe involves one part tough love and one part cheerleading. With an exercise regimen, nutritional support, supplements, essential oils, and household cleaning agents that are safe and non-toxic to address all the needs of a family from a functional and holistic perspective, I am helping them refine their health.

However, even though you may have all the strategies in your bag of tricks, you may find yourself on a different path sometimes. Imagine feeling tired, overwhelmed, over-worked, over-weight, stressed, and not knowing where to turn. Does that sound familiar? Well, that was me. I was so busy taking care of everyone else, I ended up sacrificing myself for my family and responsibilities. I was thirty pounds over-weight! However, I thought to myself, "Heather, you don't look so bad at forty-something after having two babies and not exercising at all."

Well, that was until I saw that tagged picture on social media. "Oh my god! Is that what I look like?" Yes, I was wearing a maternity shirt in the picture! I was preaching and teaching, but I had gotten so busy juggling everything, it resulted in falling off my own track. It happens to the best of us. You are not alone. The struggle is real. How could I be so healthy a few years prior and not practice what I preach? Well, the struggle of working full time in the workforce as well as running a business on your own can lead to undesired self-care.

That is where I come in. As a health coach, we are advised to come up with a specific niche. Drill down to your ideal client avatar. Since I work with all generations as a family nurse practitioner, I primarily saw struggles with weight and medical issues such as diabetes and high cholesterol in adults and teenagers of both sexes. With whom did I resonate with the most? I resonated most with busy working mothers like myself who are overwhelmed. I knew their story. I could walk the walk and talk the talk. As I became a stay-at-home mom upon my business taking off, I began to realize that all moms are overwhelmed and overworked (and underappreciated).

Women often feel like they have no idea what is going on. They feel rundown and exhausted, like they need five cups of espresso every day to just get by. They think it's normal to have no sex drive as they get older, feel tired all the time, experience issues with poop, stress levels are high, and even food sensitivities may start to appear. They may be emotional eaters who binge and are sick and tired of food being their main focus. They may be addicted to sugar. They have trouble saying "no" and feel stuck saying "yes" to everyone and everything. I assist them with boundaries and holding space for themselves. I show them what it takes every 24 hours to rise above the struggles.

As a certified health coach, I work with busy moms who struggle with their body image. I help them get their sexy back and make them feel like the woman they were before becoming a mother. When Mom gets healthy, so does her family, so I start at the source.

My children are my inspiration. I became a mother late in life (AKA the "geriatric pregnancy"). I had my first daughter at 39 years old and my second daughter at 42 years old. This is exactly why I had to change my lifestyle to ensure the ability to conceive and the safety of the pregnancy. I already had a career before having my children, but after starting a family, your priorities have to change.

My career required long days away from my children. Regretfully, I missed major stepping stones of their childhood like their first step, a haircut, playing at the park, or daycare events with families. In the 1980s, when I was a child, it was economically feasible for the mothers to stay at home. Today, both parents have to work. That doesn't necessarily mean you have to be away from your children. Like my fellow health coach Maria Forleo states, "Everything is figure-outable."

The journey as a mompreneur began in 2018 in the multi-level marketing (MLM) arena. I started a side-hustle as a wellness advocate with DoTerra, with the intention of doing more. As a nurse practitioner, we are in the western medicine arena, but I knew there was so much more I could offer besides putting a band-aid on a med-ical problem with medication. Plus, patients barely im-prove their health because they don't make the needed changes we discuss in the short 15-minute appoint-ments that we are allotted. Hence, the business name: Improve Your Tomorrow Health. As a health coach, peo-ple can improve their health with me full circle. I also started the process of certification as a holistic nutrition-ist and functional medicine provider, to completely move my practice to eastern modalities. I am growing along with my business.

Multi-level marketing is a great entry into entrepreneur-ship for moms. They sometimes get a bad reputation. However, I found organizations I was completely aligned with and used personally. Therefore, not only do I have my personal business, but I have infused MLMs which align with my wellness beliefs and practices. DoTerra, Beachbody, Thrive, and Melaleuca were the perfect fit. Additionally, I have helped other moms start their own businesses with these MLMs. They are all part of the wellness circle.

Obesity continues to rise in adults and children. Diabe-tes, hypertension, and hyperlipidemia remain out of control in the United States. I see this firsthand, which is why I am passionate about peeling the onion by work-ing with clients one on one, to help them dive into their life and health to find out why it is out of control and start to change their mindset to make habit changes to improve their health and learn how not to die!

When I was heavier, I felt like garbage, had no energy, was short of breath, and my cholesterol was elevating. I watched my fiancé struggle with cardiomyopathy, and we almost lost him. We both improved our health, and since I'd walked in the shoes of future clients, I knew this is what they needed. Lastly, it became most evident that families need help on my last trip to Disney World, I was amazed at the over-utilization of the electric power chairs used by overweight young families. The families walking were being run down at the parks by the power chairs causing more congestion in an already overly congested park. The chairs were rarely being used by the grandparents, handicapped, or injured. It was a true eye-opener of the rise of obesity and poor health of families in the United States, and it was definitely trickling down to the children.

Did I always have success in life? Let's rewind back to the 1990s and imagine bombing your SATs in high school. I was basically told I couldn't. I wouldn't get into any college. I would not amount to anything. Yes, that's right. In not so many words, a school counselor told me that. I wanted to put my head in the sand and give in to what the counselor told me. However, I took the "you can't" and turned it into a "you can," and those words became the reason I succeeded. It is hard to believe a professional woman would say that to a young, impressionable girl. However, that experience has given me the super powers to be the best.

I became the little train that could, despite the adversity I faced as a teenager. I lost my mother to ALS when I was thirteen, so I needed the full support of my father.

Unfortunately, he followed the words of the guidance counselor. "Maybe you should just become a secretary," he stated. I told myself just because I couldn't or shouldn't, I will go above and beyond. I became a registered nurse first, then completed Bachelor of Science in Nursing, then obtained a Master's of Science in Nursing and a Master's in Business Administration in Healthcare Management. Lastly, I went on to become an Advanced Practice Nurse in family medicine. That little train kept going. She became a certified health coach and certified life coach, but my education is not stopping there. I went on to create a blossoming business that helps other women and their families' health. Do not let fear be the boss of you!

The struggle appeared again when my fiancé would become aggravated with me because I was working full-time and then coming home to be a mom and house-wife as well as working on my business. Statements like, "You are always on the computer," or, "You must be talking to a boyfriend," or, "You are always doing something besides helping your family," became part of his mantra. These were all hurtful comments and certainly untrue. I was building a business and learning social media, list building, and everything else that comes with being an entrepreneur. Unfortunately, mompreneurs may not always get the needed support from their partner. The negativity can slow your process and change your mindset. I had to repeatedly discuss with him that my motivation was for both him and our children. It was so I could be home and be present.

I honestly don't think he ever comprehended how much I was doing in addition to working on a business: full-time medical provider, mom, partner, PTO (Parent Teacher Organization) vice president, kids enrolled in gymnastics and soccer. They always had clean, pressed clothes, class projects done, homework done, and lunches made by me. Holidays were created, decorated, gifted, and wrapped by me. As compared to his ex-wife who chose alcohol and drugs over his older daughter, where would he come up with these comments about me?

Men do not realize how much we do. Parenting is full of sacrifices and struggles whether you have a partner or not. Perhaps, instead of judging, he could have appreciated and understood my efforts and started to take care of some of the responsibilities that should be shared by both parents so it did not appear that I was always working. Eventually, he began to understand why I was always so busy back then, but he still displayed some of the negative comments that would bring my motivation down and increase my frustration. Ironically, he likes to take naps, enjoys sitting on the couch watching television, or working on his car, but that did not make me comment negatively toward him. We needed the help of counseling to overcome these struggles. As a result of this, I will be sure to provide continual support and motivation to my daughters.

I recently attended a motivational speaking engagement about the five love languages from Gary Chapman. I learned about a tool that could be used for anyone in your family to communicate better. I would advise taking their quiz before starting your mompreneur journey. I wish had known about this earlier because it sure improved our relationship in recent time. Visit www.5lovelanguages.com to take the quiz. Believe me, it will help all the relationships in your family (husband, children, and teenagers). Mompreneurship may be easy for some, a struggle for others, and some moms are completely alone starting their journey. Be prepared for some ups and downs.

I know the school system has changed for the better, but as adults, this proves we must be careful how we speak to our children and teenagers. My story could have been a lot different and set up for failure. Sometimes, you have to speak to your partner and explain your end goal (your why beneath the why). They may support you or they may not. Include them in your journey. Discuss your ideas and make them feel included. The key is to truly keep the lines of communication open to prevent obstacles in your business journey.

It is amazing that negativity from the guidance counselor molded my mindset positively at sixteen. I had no clue it was happening then, but now that I look back, that one statement pushed me to strive and I am thankful. The journey of mompreneurship has not been easy, but I just kept brushing myself off and trying again. My business started off a tad slower than expected because clients often prefer to medicate a medical problem instead of preventing or halting it. I had to pivot and look through a different lens as to how I could help people better. This is the importance of showing up, no matter what obstacles get in your way.

To overcome the "roadblocks" that come into life, start by changing your mindset to succeed instead. Mindset is a mental attitude or inclination and a fixed state of mind. If I had to choose a word that always resonated with me, it would be perseverance. It is a continued effort to do or achieve something despite difficulties, failure, or opposition. That has been the story of my life. Unfortunately, as women, we must overcome roadblocks throughout our life, so this is an ongoing process.

Internal resources of success included my end goal to be home with my family. My children were and always will be my motivation for everything I do. Striving towards that goal with perseverance and discipline got me there. External resources included my faith, going for walks to reframe my mindset when roadblocks occurred, family support, and support from fellow health coaches who were going through similar struggles. I focused on my vision board daily to help me get in the right mindset. Wake up early and start on the right foot. How you start your morning sets the tone for the rest of the day.

Mindset is the ultimate reason we get through the adversity. We need to reframe our mental attitude to reach our goals. Through positive affirmations and perseverance, the adversity made me stronger to reach my goals and help serve the population I intended to help. It is my story of overcoming struggles and how mindset was changed for success in getting a business off the ground on my own, while working full-time and being a mom with all the responsibilities that come with that. If you are reading this, then I am sure you know what I am talking about!

My takeaway with this experience is to keep striving for your goal, no matter the struggles and roadblocks that appear along the journey. Set your mind and you will succeed. Think of your journey like crossing a river. The water may be rough or cold, the rocks you walk across may be slippery, and you may or may not have someone holding your hand. Just keep your eyes on the prize of getting to the other side (where the goal awaits you) and your mind and heart will get you there.

Not getting the support from those you expect it from is disheartening. I would advise finding external support such as faith, self-belief techniques for motivation, or support of other like-minded people. Find your tribe and don't be afraid to lean on them. That is one of the reasons I also created a health coach starter program which is marketed to new health coaches. They need support and tips to start their businesses because it isn't always easy. I advise starting by getting clarity with whom you serve and the problems you solve. If this is not narrowed down when starting a business, it is impossible to get started correctly. Also, a successful mompreneur business is usually based on your story. So much money goes to the grave, such as ideas or inventions that were never implemented, stories that were never told, or books that were never written. Only you have the power to turn the page on your story.

Unfortunately, it doesn't stop at lack of support. Some mainstream struggles of starting your mompreneurship may include lack of funding, mommy guilt, imposter syndrome, not being taken seriously, battling stereotypes, and struggling to juggle it all. Many mompreneurs are young (in their twenties), and I started my journey as a middle aged woman, so I struggled with that stereotype of being "too old." I worked full time and started my business, which was a struggle. I wish I'd made better financial decisions starting the business. I help other moms not make the same mistakes and fall for the dangling carrot that will boost a business, because not all systems were worth the investment. Not all moms want to work alone, so collaboration with other like-minded moms when starting your journey may lighten the load of responsibility. Choose your team or partners wisely, as your business is your baby. Outline agreements in writing in the early stages of your business.

I encourage mompreneurs to balance a few key concepts to have success in their business and avoid burnout. It is difficult to balance paid and unpaid work. Utilize time management strategies, so it is not all work and no play. I've found it helpful to only have three tasks per day on my list. Complete all three and move on. Make sure at least one of the three to-do items includes a money-making task every day. Plan your week in advance and set your goals for efficiency. Honor your time and that of others. Know when it is time to unplug. Know when it is time to outsource and have workflow systems in place. You do not have to do everything. Create a rolodex of resources that can help. Have realistic expectations for yourself, without being hard on yourself. Remember that personal sacrifice will occur when building a business, so try to always make time for self-care and avoid overwhelm. Be true to your vision and your mission (your why) and build your village with a community of trust.

I love to support moms. My health coaching focuses on moms. In some way, we are all a hot mess, so I have "hot mess mom" groups because the struggle of a new body image after motherhood is something that most do not talk about. I offer support and tips. Some moms are lucky and get their original body back. That is not the majority of mothers, though. We sacrifice ourselves for our families. We need to embrace getting our sexy back and feeling like ourselves again. Feeling sexy is so empowering. Moms feel like they need to be so granola and can't feel sexy. They feel ashamed of being attractive, like it is unholy. It is time for self-love. We have to stop being afraid and/or guilty to take care of ourselves for once. Guess what? A Healthy Mom = A Healthy Family.

Who am I? I am your new best friend, the forty-something-year-old from Jersey. That's why I give my clients a combination of tough love and cheerleading. I am full of enthusiasm to help moms because I have been there. My strategies are true and tried. Although our struggles may not be the same, I will meet you where you are at. Most of my clients start with me, but never leave my inner circle. They sometimes need additional hand-holding after a program. Once the learning and transitions starts, clients get as excited as I am about what is taught and want to know more. I am very supportive to women, and sometimes, that is all they need and stick with me. I am here for you. Let me help you with one of the various programs or products which are provided in person or online. I do recognize that not all clients want to work one-on-one. Some do better in groups or at their own pace alone. If something doesn't work as expected, we could pivot and try another approach because our bodies are unique. Some people benefit with one session, while another may want a three-month package. We all have unique situations or support at home and learn differently. This is why I created many packages compared to other health coaches.

I teach moms how to remove toxins from life, lose weight, gain health, and more. You may ask why I mention toxins so much. We are already over-exposed in unpreventable ways via the air we breathe and what we absorb through our skin, so I help moms discover ways they can decrease the toxic overload and feel better. "Am I toxic?" you ask. We all are in toxic overload. Some people have many symptoms of it, others may have no symptoms at all. If that is not reason enough to start a program, as the rapper Ice Cube says, "You better check yourself, before you wreck yourself." As moms, we do everything to ensure a safe pregnancy, so don't stop there. Keep yourself and your family healthy. My journey to remove toxins from lives is based on my mother's death related to ALS. Her sister died of it, too. I am convinced that the disease was triggered by toxins.

There are so many unique avenues we could work on together to improve your health and that of your family. I offer a free discovery session and meet you where you are at. If I am the right fit, then we can explore a wonderful journey together. Otherwise, I would be happy to give you recommendations. Either way, take charge of your life and your body. Think of it as an outfit, but it can only be worn once. Why not make the best of it?

We can't just rely on western medicine any longer. We need to embrace the eastern modalities I incorporate and start preventing disease. That is where I come in. I have the expertise of the medical, nutritional, coaching, and functional approaches. In the functional world, we refer to disease as dis-ease because everything is reversible and the body is asking for help when it is not at ease. Our life choices determine the biochemistry of our body. Will the body go down the wellness road or the disease road? Just because a disease is in your family, does not mean the gene will go that route unless you let it. Prevention is key. However, even if such diseases are already in play, we could potentially reverse them.

I know that I am not alone. All moms have many struggles. It might be health or weight. It could be how to start a mompreneurship. It could be your family's health. Say yes to yourself for once. Your future self will be forever grateful.

About the Author

Heather Zeveney has been a Registered Nurse since 1998 and became an Advanced Practice Nurse in 2010. She holds a Masters of Science in Nursing and Masters of Business in Healthcare Administration since 2006. She started her business Improve Your Tomorrow Health in 2018 because she saw there was a need to do more to improve health of patients besides prescribing medication. She started her healthy journey prior to this by eating clean and removing toxins from her home because she wanted to start having children and wanted to keep her animals healthy. These changes allowed easy conception late in life, healthy pregnancy and delivery, weight loss, improved health, and she also decreased her partner's heart disease. She strives to continue to help others do the same. She joined DoTerra as a Wellness Advocate and became a Certified Health and Life Coach. She also incorporates additional modalities with clients using BEACHBODY coaching for exercise, Lev-el Thrive supplements for energy, and

Melaleuca for toxin-free home cleaning agents. Her journey continues for Certification as a Holistic Nutritionist and Functional Medicine Practitioner. She offers programs and products in-person or online addressing the many issues of health in today's world including sugar addiction, toxic life, immunity, and more. She loves helping mothers regain their health and confidence and then strives to help the family as well. A Healthy Mom = A Healthy Family. Heather has an energetic personality and is a lifelong New Jersey resident that enjoys her shore life and the outdoors. Please visit her website to learn more about her programs and/or book a free discovery session at:

www.improveyourtomorrowhealth.com

and any further questions contact her at

heather@improveyourtomorrowhealth.com

Here is a wonderful freebie to begin healthy habits to improve health in just 5 days!!

Visit http://www.improveyourtomorrowhealth.info/go

CHAPTER SIX

This Was Not What I Planned, But Plans Change

By Lynne Getz

I'm not one of those women who always wanted to be a mother. As a little girl, I played with dolls, and pretended to be a mom, but even while playing pretend, I was a mom who left and went to work. I started babysitting when I was 12 because I wanted to buy a pair of over-priced Guess jeans. I took a babysitting course at the local YMCA, and I read all The Babysitter's Club Books. I put together a babysitting kit, which was a bag filled with games, coloring books, crayons, and other fun projects. I totally looked the part. I would show up at the house, babysitting kit in hand, and 30 minutes after the parents left I was counting down the minutes until bedtime so I could watch TV and call my friends.

In my mid-20s I was a recruiter for a healthcare consulting and research firm. During interviews, I'd ask candidates to tell me about their goals. Their answers would give me perspective into how they saw the job fitting into their overall plan for their lives. It helped me determine if they had the potential for long-term growth with the company, or if they were simply looking for something to include on their resume before the next shiny opportunity came along.

Or at least, I was naive enough to think it did.

The truth is that life rarely goes according to plan. If you'd asked me in those interviews where I saw my career going, I would have given you a well-scripted answer about how I was looking to gain the skills necessary to rise up to the next level of client management, gaining more responsibility and becoming an expert in my field and landing some snazzy title like Managing Director.

Basically, I would have fed you a load of bullshit.

If you had you asked me years ago if I would be a "mompreneur" I likely would have laughed out loud and spit out my drink at the idea. Me? An entrepreneur? Is this a trick question? Being an entrepreneur definitely wasn't part of the plan, but plans change.

My first big change of plans came when I learned I was pregnant for the first time just before my 29th birthday. At the same time, my husband and I had made the decision to relocate for his job from the DC area to Charlotte, NC. The warm weather and lower cost of living made the choice easy, but I wasn't sure what this move would mean for my career.

In the year before becoming pregnant, I transitioned from field consulting into human resources because I was tired of being a road warrior. (Also, it's really hard to get pregnant when you're traveling 75% of the time.) I wasn't sure if I wanted to stay in HR, and I knew that with a baby on the way I couldn't go back on the road. So I made the decision not to look for a new job until after the baby was born. I knew I was marketable and I knew how to nail an interview, so I told myself I'd find a great job even if I was unemployed for a short time.

My pregnancy had been mostly uneventful. The move had gone well, and I was enjoying the luxury of not working during my pregnancy. I felt ready, and so when I went into labor four weeks early, I wasn't worried.

The first indication that anything was wrong with my son happened minutes after his arrival. I told my husband to get the camera and get some pictures of him while the doctors were cleaning and weighing him, but they stopped him from taking photos.

"He's having some trouble breathing," they said as they shooed him away from the corner of the room where they had my son.

A few minutes later, they wheeled my son past me in an incubator, telling us he was to be admitted to the Neonatal Intensive Care Nursery (NICN).

In the weeks that followed, doctors detailed the many abnormalities my son, Bobby, had. I would ask questions, but no one knew why he was presenting with so many challenges. Just before his discharge we were given an answer. My son had a rare chromosome deletion on the short arm of his sixth chromosome. At the time of diagnosis, we were told he was one of only twelve in the world with his condition.

After 35 days in the NICN, Bobby was discharged. There were multiple specialists we had to see and therapies we had to schedule. In addition to becoming a mom, I had become a care coordinator. Each day I had new appointments to schedule, new therapies to research, and new information to digest. He had multiple surgeries within his first six months, and it became clear that he would never lead a typical life.

It was also becoming increasingly clear that my role in our family was going to become being a caregiver. We had moved for my husband's career, and I had left mine. At the time when we had made that decision we were equal earners at similar levels in our respective companies, a fact I was proud of. I never wanted to be a woman who relied on her husband for financial support. But now, here I was, in the role I'd never intended to play - a full-time, stay-at-home mom and housewife. Another change of plans. And in this role I became depressed, anxious, and overwhelmed.

In the years that followed I started working part-time, thanks to help from my mother-in-law with babysitting and then my son's enrollment in a specialized preschool.

I went back to working for my former company, and my depression lessened. I felt like myself again.

But it wasn't a career. It was a job. I had gone back to the same position and the same pay, and since I was part-time, there wasn't an opportunity to advance.

A few years after having my second child, Katie, my husband was once again offered a promotion in another city. This time our move would take us back up north, to Philadelphia. I was excited to head north again. While I enjoyed the mild winters I had never quite adapted to being a southern girl, although I do throw out an occasional y'all now and then. I also wasn't thrilled with the schools in our area. While the United States does have provisions in the Individuals with Disabilities Education Act (IDEA) for students like Bobby, there are many aspects of that law that are left to interpretation by individual states and school districts.

I maintained my part-time job throughout the move, but it was challenging. I no longer had my mother-in-law five minutes away to call when I needed back-up childcare, and my primary childcare was also more expensive. I found myself working fewer and fewer hours. And then, I found out I was pregnant with our third child.

I wanted a third child. After the birth of my oldest, I had made it clear that we were either having two more children or we were done. That's a long and complicated story for another memoir, but I was adamant that if we gave our son siblings, there needed to be two.

But I was burnt out. My marriage was struggling, I was finding it hard to make friends in a new city, and I wasn't doing my job well in the limited time I had. And so, with all things considered, I made the decision to leave my former company for good.

Once again, I was a full-time, stay-at-home mom, and once again, I was miserable. During one of many breakdowns I had while talking with one of my friends, she said, "If you want to take care of your kids, you have to take care of their mom." That was the truth I needed to hear. I'd been so busy supporting the lives of everyone around me that I'd forgotten that what I needed to do was to take care of myself.

Shortly after my third child, Ben, was born, I was invited to a jewelry party by the newborn photographer I'd used to take pictures of Ben. I fell in love with the unique pieces that told stories, and started to ask questions about the company. It was the first time I had been introduced to direct sales. I'd attended parties in the past, but I'd never sat down and looked at how the business worked. I was open to something new and I wanted the chance to get out and meet new people, and this seemed like a great way to do it!

In October of 2012 I launched my first direct selling business. At first, I reached out mostly to friends and family and posted pictures to Facebook. I gained some customers, but knew that if I really wanted to grow, I needed to expand my circle and meet new people. I started to look for networking organizations in my area.

Networking opened up a whole new world to me. In these groups I discovered there were women like me running all kinds of businesses. There were other direct sellers and network marketers, realtors, financial managers, brick and mortar store owners, service providers, photographers, and more. I would attend these meetings and they made me feel something that I hadn't felt since becoming a mom: connected and valued for who I was outside of motherhood.

After a while, I realized the thing lighting me up wasn't me talking about my jewelry business. Instead, it was connecting with the other women, and connecting them with each other. I became known as the person who could always give a referral, and my network appreciated the support.

I soon found a home in a networking group called Bizzy Mamas, a small, local group started by two moms. They built the Bizzy Mamas group to support mompreneurs through a mostly online community that was complemented by in-person events. The moms I met through that group were the people I'd been searching for since becoming a mother. These were women like me, who needed more than motherhood.

In 2015 I said goodbye to my direct sales business. My first career out of college had been in radio and I missed working in the media, so I ventured back into broadcasting and started a show called Mom to Mom. The show's goal was to connect local moms to local resources and to each other, and featured interviews with mompreneurs on various subjects from starting a business, giving make-up tips, and navigating early intervention, to dealing with postpartum depression. It was my passion project! But while the show gave me a platform to showcase others, it didn't give me the opportunity to showcase myself.

I brainstormed about what else I wanted to do. The more I thought about who I was, the more I found I didn't fit into one single box. I'm a stay-at-home mom. I run a home-based business. I'm an awesome friend. I'm an advocate for my son and other children with special needs. I love to share the realness of my life, and how I try my best to live with passion and purpose. But I also totally fuck-up sometimes. I'm not the best wife, and there are days that I don't exactly love this motherhood thing. I'm all of these things. So, I started writing about all of it, and my blog, 'Like A Mother,' was born.

My self-proclaimed media blitz continued when my friend and I came up with an idea to start a podcast, talking about motherhood while drinking in the closet. Liz and Lynne on the Rocks debuted on iTunes in 2017 to rave reviews! Each episode centered around a cocktail we'd named to complement the theme of the show. Our fans listening while waiting in the carpool line called it genius. I was finally doing the things I loved, but there was one problem - I wasn't making money.

Finding sponsors and putting out the content they want is a full-time job in itself, and unless you have a ginormous following, it's one that doesn't pay well. I dove into the world of sponsored content and I hated it. The work didn't feel authentic. I was making pennies for the amount of time I was dedicating to my media endeavors. And because I wasn't making any money with my projects, my husband became less supportive.

Little did I know that the opportunity I was waiting for was just around the corner. A friend from my networking group had been asked to help launch a new direct sales company, and I was one of the first people she told about it. I was also one of the first people to say, "No thanks. I don't think that's for me." But I promised to support her in her new endeavor, and a few weeks later when she hosted a preview party for the product, I showed up to cheer her on. Then, I tried the product, and I was sold!

I never intended to go back to direct selling, but hey, plans change, remember? I knew this product was going to be huge, and I wanted to be part of it. I had no idea if I would be successful. I hated sales and I had floundered in direct selling before, but the business kit cost was reasonable so I jumped in.

It's officially been three years since I launched this direct sales business, and what a ride it's been. I've had challenges in my personal life, including the unexpected passing of my father, multiple hospitalizations for Bobby, and a diagnosis of dyslexia for Katie. Despite these things, my business thrived. I grew a team of amazing consultants, and in August of 2020 our team's lifetime sales volume surpassed $11 million. My monthly income is more than I ever made in consulting or recruiting, and my business has allowed me to regain my prior confidence, to find purpose in helping other men and women succeed, and to be the woman I know I'm meant to be while still being the mom I need to be.

I know there are naysayers out there who look down on direct sales and discourage women from getting involved. I'm not going to deny that some people in multi-level marketing businesses operate without morals and use tactics that, quite frankly, suck. And when that happens, it makes everyone in the industry look bad. But there are people in every industry who do their jobs in a way that makes their field look bad. Ever heard a lawyer joke? Know any lawyers who aren't ambulance-chasing snakes? Yes? Me too. In fact, most of the lawyers I know are honest and moral business men and women. Honestly, I don't think I've ever actually met an ambulance chaser.

However, I've met honest, hard-working, strong and wonderful people through my experiences with direct sales. My philosophy around how I coach my team is pretty simple: don't be a jerk. Treat people the way you want to be treated in business and in life, no matter what business you're in. It's a simple philosophy that has helped me to simultaneously build my business and my friendships.

Life definitely hasn't gone according to plan, but that's not a bad thing. The farther I go down the path of being a mompreneur, the more grateful I am that life has brought me here. If an interviewer asked me today where I saw myself five years from now, I'd tell them that I hope my life has as much joy as it has now, and that it continues to have balance between being a mom and being me. I pray for more opportunities for creativity and connection, and I believe my earning potential will continue to be limitless.

Because that's the beauty of being your own boss and having your own business. Your journey is yours, and the path you follow can only lead you where you let it take you.

Maybe that 12-year-old me with the babysitting kit knew what she was getting into after all. She wasn't practicing to be a mom. She was practicing to be a mompreneur.

About the Author

Lynne Getz is a married mom of three living in the outskirts of Philly whose life can be summed up in six words: this is not what I planned. Her first child was born with a rare chromosome disorder, so she became a different kind of mom than she ever expected.

She started her blog, Like a Mother (www.belikeamother.com), to show other moms that motherhood and martyrdom are not synonymous, that self-care is not selfish, and that having a child with multiple disabilities does not mean you have to sacrifice your goals--you just have to adjust them.

In 2017 she signed on with a direct sales company (after swearing that direct sales just wasn't her thing) and found a new way to help busy moms find their sparkle by sharing an incredible product and business opportunity. She quickly rose to the top ranks of her company, and she was invited to speak to the other leaders at their 2018 National Conference.

Her writing has been syndicated on Reality Moms and Her View From Home and published in The Unofficial Guidebook to Surviving Life With Teenagers. She was also a featured speaker at the Pivot and Make Waves Virtual Women's Conference.

Above all, her most important job is teaching her children to be good people.

Connect with Lynne Getz:

You can find Lynne sharing her thoughts, tips, musings, memes, and coffee selfies on social media. Follow @lynnegetz on Facebook, Instagram, Twitter, and TikTok. For media and speaking inquiries, visit www.lynnegetz.com.

CHAPTER SEVEN

Constantly Bouncing Back: Getting Used to 'New Normals'

By Jennifer St John

I turn the key in the charming wooden door of my studio. Even this small action puts a smile on my face. Opening this door makes me feel alive! I feel alive in a way I haven't felt in a long time. The ink on the lease agreement is only a month old, but things are coming along nicely. A small renovation refreshed the space and transformed the six hundred square feet into a working studio and office space. Sunlight streams through the large glass windows at the front of the street-level building. For an artisan, it's the kind of natural light you fall in love with.

I say, "Hi, Mom and Dad," as I pass an oversized picture of my parents. It was taken in the seventies. They are young; Mom is laughing, and my dad has his tongue stuck out. I love this picture of them. With this space, I am in the next phase of launching my business, "Marnie & Michael," an artisan shop meets mental health initiative. My mom was undiagnosed and untreated with mental illness until her early fifties. She had become a mother at seventeen years old, so our entire life has been affected by her mental health struggles. My business is my way of "paying it forward."

This isn't my first rodeo as a business owner. Still, it is an entirely different experience with two children in tow (one of whom has higher-than-average needs) and a husband who's barely around due to his work schedule. I have a powerful desire to have an identity outside of my wife/partner/mother roles, and I know I must find a way to make this work. If it's not too much to ask for, having time for a little self-care would be nice!

I have been artistic from a young age and was always a keen student. Mom had drilled into my head that college was the way to go—get an actual skill so you can be employable. I did a three-year Interior Design program, and then I was spat out into the world to start at the bottom. I worked my ass off at a tremendous commercial design firm and didn't heed the warnings of wiser co-workers to make sure I didn't burn out—which, of course, I did.

With my interest in film making and my design background, I secured two internships at a local film and television production company—one in the art department and one as a Producer Assistant. I fell in love with the business side of Producing and was soon starting my film and television company with my business partner, Erin. Over the next several years, we produced projects for both regional and national broadcasters, successfully raising and managing six-figure budgets and distributing content around the world.

I did all of this while trying to manage my relationship with my mom. Our childhood was exceptionally chaotic and traumatic, leaving my sisters and me with a significant weight to carry from a young age. The mania consuming Mom resulted in drastic highs and lows. All anyone could see were her unhealthy coping mechanisms of drugs, alcohol, and reckless relationships. We grew up surrounded by shame and secrecy, never being able to share the reality of our situation with anyone fully. My dad tried to hang on with love and babies, but it slipped through his fingers. He would continue to reconcile with her for the rest of our childhood, at times successful but always short-lived.

Before I left home, we'd had eighteen different addresses, and I attended eight different schools in two different countries. Nothing felt constant or stable in our lives. In her unhealthy state, Mom was very good at getting us involved in fighting her battles and always made sure we took her side. It usually meant coercing us to turn on someone we loved, like our father, my older sister, or a family member. I honed an intense "flight or fight" instinct, learned the art of fierce independence, took myself very seriously, and continuously sought people's approval, all while never fully trusting anyone.

In adulthood, it felt like my relationship with Mom was always in "push-and-pull" mode. She would go from leaving me crying, feeling like shit to then filling me with love. When I was twenty years old, she was in a car accident while driving intoxicated and ended up breaking her neck. As usual, she wasn't charged, which was infuriating and dangerous as her behaviors grew in audacity and frequency. My oldest sister was pregnant and spent the three-hour drive to the hospital preparing herself to potentially deal with the family members of someone Mom had injured or killed. During her recovery, Mom asked me through her tears how it was possible that my sisters and I were still by her side. This was the closest she ever came to taking responsibility for the trauma and abuse we experienced growing up. I had high hopes this was her "rock bottom," but I was wrong.

I went to Al-Anon and began to process things. The first thing I did was rebuild my relationship with my dad and my oldest sister. It took time, many conversations, and much courage, love, and forgiveness, but we got there. Slowly, grandchildren were becoming a part of the picture, and as things with Mom continued to not get better, some of my sisters became fearful of history repeating itself. Out of desperation, we all started to set healthy boundaries. Some of us went small. For example, visits with grandchildren weren't alone anymore. Some of us went big; I stopped all communication with Mom for almost two years.

I felt like I had no other choice. It was either her or me. It had to be done for self-preservation. I had stopped counting the number of times we had begged her to get help. As young as six, seven, or eight years old, we would gather together and ask her to get better. We didn't know what "better" meant, but we knew we wanted our lives to be different. Now, as adults, most of us had finally gained enough strength to put ourselves first and say, "Enough."

During these years apart, Mom was diagnosed correctly with Bi-Polar, OCD, PTSD, and adult ADHD. With therapy, she moved from being a victim of childhood trauma herself to becoming a survivor. It was her tallest mountain to climb, but it's one that fills me with pride. When I saw Mom almost two years later at my uncle's funeral, I barely recognized her. She blew me away with her transformation, and it became the bridge for us to start to heal our relationship. We both had grown to learn to forgive people who were never going to apologize. By taking responsibility for her mental health, she was becoming the person she had always wanted to be, the kind of grandmother her grandchildren would never have to "recover" from. Mom and Dad reconciled again, and this time, decades later, for good.

When I was 33 years old, we had our first child, our son Lawson. Even though Canada has maternity leave subsidies, as a business owner, I knew I wouldn't be able to take much time off. It wasn't realistic. We were in production and had a film crew shooting for a documentary project. I was signing cheques for payroll while breastfeeding one-week-old Lawson. I was feeling great, though, and was so excited to start the parenting/business juggle.

When Lawson was eight weeks old, I went back to work part-time and continued to teach part-time. Our producing fees were calculated by a strict formula of percentages in the budget, and budgets seemed to be getting smaller and smaller, even though it took the same teams and services to pull them off as it had five years prior. As owners of each film, the idea was to offset our low production fees with international sales across multiple platforms. Enter 2008/2009, combined with the advent of digital content and dwindling financing options available, and this business model was breaking—fast. To me, it was starting to feel more like a glorified hobby, and when you can't pay your daycare bill with your income, you know something has to give.

Adding to all of this, Lawson was twelve months old and still not sleeping solidly. My cognitive abilities were not the same, and I felt like the walking dead—I wasn't myself and was not on top of everything I needed to be.

In our desperation, we hired a "Sleep Expert" to come wave a magic wand and tell us what we were doing wrong! The damn rod didn't work.

Now thirty-six and pregnant with our second child, we still had the distribution phase of our last project to complete. Even after a big push in the US to dozens of independent theatres, international sales were a no-go. We were hanging on by our fingernails at this point and had to close our doors. We were so disappointed that we couldn't find a way to make things work. It felt like the end of an era for us.

My pregnancy with Nora was tough. If I thought I was tired before, I had now entered a level of tiredness I didn't know existed. I felt alone on the parenting front with Murray gone for work all the time. The last thing I wanted to do was add something to my plate right now, but I had noticed Lawson was struggling. Transitions of any kind were stressful for him, and he wasn't meeting some social milestones. Lawson could focus on one thing for an extended period to his detriment. Emotionally, he was empathetic, frequently afraid of his own shadow. It broke my heart every time Lawson was pulled out of my arms at daycare drop-offs. He spent a lot of time under tables, as most environments felt too loud and filled with too many people for him.

One night, at swimming lessons, he escalated from, "Mom, I don't want to swim anymore," to having a meltdown to uncontrollably sobbing to then, shockingly, punching me in the head several times as I tried to move him through the packed lobby. You could hear a pin drop. I knew I had to stay calm and defuse the situation, but I also knew my heart had just broken into tiny pieces, and I was not going to live like this. We immediately took steps to have him formally assessed.

The official diagnosis became Autism Spectrum Disorder (ASD), specifically, Asperger's exceptionality. Every child with this is different, which means every treatment plan is different. Just when you feel like you've figured it all out, everything changes. He gets older or there's a change in the environment or puberty starts or the wind blows in a different direction, you name it, it changes. I felt like we finally had a road map, and I could work with that. At least it gave us a direction. I immersed myself in books, websites, online support groups, local resources, anything I could get my hands on. I was always reading, learning, researching.

Through all of this, Mom was one of my biggest lifelines. She and Dad now lived just down the road from us, and we didn't go many days without a connection. On top of that, Mom was amazing with Lawson, and he adored her. She had the patience and love to be fully in the moment with him. As he grew, he very much looked forward to his "Grandma days." When Nora came along, Mom was right by my side again. She basked in her Grandma role and thoroughly enjoyed all her grandchildren. Mom was her healthiest by far—mentally, emotionally, and physically, even entering half-marathon walks. She was living her best life, full of mindfulness, love, and joy.

Finding a school for Lawson proved difficult until I found a new start-up in our area. The school was small and very much about each student—academically, physically, and emotionally. For children on the Autism Spectrum, school is such a big part of the puzzle, and we felt like we were off to the races having found this match made in heaven!

I've always said, "Sleep equals sanity." I was starting to feel sane again! Lawson was now taking a sleep aid, and I was getting more stretches of uninterrupted rest. I was feeling like myself again. I was even finding time for some self-care. I started to run and moved from ten-kilometer lengths to half-marathons, and I was back at the gym doing weight training, too. It had been years since I felt this good.

With Lawson settled into school and Nora doing her combo daycare/Grandma days, it felt like I could finally take some time to spread my wings again. I knew I would be a business owner still, but I just didn't know what that was going to look like. I realized I wanted to work with my hands and create a viable creative business, so I leaned on my background to design patterns for a line of handmade leather bags. I taught myself how to hand stitch leather through YouTube videos and I created several prototypes. The feedback was very positive, so I started working with a local company that provided one-on-one business development plans for artisans. We met weekly for three-hour sessions, and I embraced this development phase of my new venture.

I don't know how to describe this next phase in our lives. Maybe "detonation"? Sometimes words can't fully summarize the shift that happens, and losing three close family members in less than a year is one of those times.

Mom, Dad, and one of my aunts all passed away.

They were all just gone.

Mom had been given a terminal cancer diagnosis in May, and we thought we might have four to six months. We actually had ten weeks. I poured my heart out to her in letters which she read over and over, and on the night before she finally slipped into the last stages of dying, when she could no longer read, she just held them. I was so angry she wasn't getting more time. Why?? She had worked so God damn hard to dig herself out of a gigantic hole and now this?

We all just wrapped our arms around each other, including my dad. We inched our way through a "year of firsts" after Mom passed away, going through all the ups and downs grief takes you on. Less than ten months after saying goodbye to the love of his life, my dad literally died from a broken heart. While we held his hand in the hospital as he coded multiple times, he whispered, "I'm sorry."

We had lost family members in the past, but this was different. I wasn't just dealing with my grief this time since my entire extended family was also slowly putting things back together. Lawson and Nora were just devastated. Afraid and in pain, they slept with Murray and me for months, crying themselves to sleep. Their childhood innocence was gone, replaced with the knowledge that everyone they knew was going to die at some point.

With the first anniversary of losing Dad upon us, we decided to move closer to immediate family again. Now more than ever, family was at the top of our list. We knew it was a significant change, especially for Lawson and Nora, but I strongly felt the pros outweighed the cons. After a lot of research on the schools in our new area, we settled on a house. We wanted to ensure the new school would have support available to help Lawson navigate. Nora was as social as ever and ready to take on life at any moment! She was so looking forward to having a larger friend circle.

Business-wise, I was struggling to get traction. I had been inching along but wasn't ready to fully put up my "OPEN" sign yet. There was a lot of fear there. Was I going to have the time? Was I going to have the energy? Was I ready? What other personal setbacks were going to disrupt things again? Some of my friends couldn't understand what was taking me so long, and I was beginning to wonder. Could I do this myself? Am I being realistic? Am I being too selfish?

I decided to make this move a fresh start. I needed to push myself forward, so after we all settled into the house and the kids started school, I went after an opening in a shared studio space. After applying, interviewing, and being accepted, I was elated. I was so excited to be working with a group of creative professionals again. I craved this environment and the feedback of like-minded individuals. I also found a great yoga studio nearby and moved self-care back towards the top of my list. Nora was flourishing, and considering what a significant change this was, Lawson was doing well, too. Murray and I were pinching ourselves.

Then the wheels fell off again.

Things slowly began to crumble for Lawson. His sensory reactions were high again, and socially, he went from playing with friends at recess to pacing by himself on the yard to then hiding under the steps of the portable, counting down the seconds until he could go back into his classroom. Scared all the time, he was now hyperventilating and having full-on panic attacks.

We had already experienced so much with Lawson, but seeing him gripped with fear to the point of not being able to breathe or move was an entirely new level of anxiety. It was so distressing for the whole family and challenging for Nora's seven-year-old heart and head to absorb. After some emergency appointments, he was diagnosed further with Social Anxiety Disorder (SAD), and once again, everything was different.

Here I was, yet again in a situation out of my control, and there was no way around it. I had a little pity-party for myself the day I pulled out of the shared artisan space. There was just no way I was going to be able to fit that into my life right now. The journey back to "normal" (whatever that was going to look like) was going to take months or years. We were being prepared by Lawson's team of professionals for this to be a long road. I felt like I was always the one bending, the one taking a step back and putting myself last. There were days I wanted to scream, "Why me?"

Then I did what I always do. I dove in and researched and listened and read and reached out. I found a local therapist who Lawson saw several times a week. Medication started, and doctor appointments were set routinely for check-ins. The dance between triggers, pushing himself, and coping began. He slowly began to leave his room, then leave the house, then get in the car, then get out of the car at school, and then finally, go through the front doors—all the simple tasks we had taken for granted before.

I was running purely on adrenaline. The weight of our day-to-day lives felt enormous to me. This included making sure Nora's needs were still being met, and she was thriving. This included trying to have a strong and connected marriage when both Murray and I had zero time or energy left at the end of each day or week (divorce rates for parents of high needs children is above the national average). This included surrounding ourselves with caring and understanding friends and family who didn't make us feel like shit when plans changed at the last minute or when visits were cut short or we couldn't join certain events because of sensory issues (too loud, too many people, the waitress is wearing too much metal jewelry, etc.) or there were too many panic attacks that day.

There's also the simple fact that some days, you have to pick your battles.

At one of his Occupational Therapy appointments, I had to continually pull his grip from around my neck for over ten minutes as he tried to stay close and not let me go. Almost out the door, I looked down at him lying on the ground, hands now wrapped around my ankles for dear life, tears streaming down his face. "Please don't leave me," he sobbed. He was in full-on "flight mode."

"Are you okay?" the therapist kept asking me. "Am I okay?" I asked myself.

This scene felt surreal yet so familiar. I realized Lawson had been in this same position since he was a toddler, always seeking my anchoring touch, my endless love, and my constant encouragement. The strength this took on all levels—physical, mental, and emotional—this IS my normal. I will always dig as deep as I must for him. This is his normal, too. He has already done more work to learn how to be in this world than most adults I know! As a friend of mine said recently, "You may see us struggle, but you will never see us quit!"

Once the acute stages of SAD were behind us, I started to notice some spaces for rent in our little town. "Why not open a studio here?" I thought. Rent was very reasonable, and there was a space available within walking distance to the school, minutes from home, and close to all the specialists. Murray completely supported me, and after seeing a space, we jumped on it.

I struggled with a name for my new company for a while, but with all our recent life events, it became apparent to me. When you lose a loved one, one of the first things you notice is, over time, people stop saying their names out loud. "Marnie & Michael" is perfect, and now I get to say my parents' names every day.

Things have come a long way from when I was a ten-year-old kid asking when Mom was coming home so I could feel loved. Mental health is still a phrase which makes people uncomfortable. Although things have changed since I was a child, they still have a very long way to go. With our mental health initiative, we're providing a place where people with this shared experience can honestly and openly share their written stories of loving a family member with a mental health challenge.

It took many, many, many years, but I do feel my mom and I came to a very loving and respectful place in the last decade of her life. I'm forever grateful that my children only ever knew her joy. Mom always wanted to be a writer. To honor this wish, I've curated a collection of our journal entries and letters to one another into a project entitled "Be Kind, Love Hard, Make Memories: A Guided Journal Meets Mini Memoir". I hope this little story of ours assists others in their experience—one of survival, coping, and most importantly, healing.

"Marnie & Michael" finally came together when I realized I had to make my business work for my life, not make my life work for my business. This venture is different because I'm different, and my life is different. My definition of success has changed, too. One day soon, success will mean having a team hired, multiple bag lines launched, and product selling across the country! Most days right now, success is getting Lawson to school past first recess or getting into the studio for five hours, or fitting in a yoga class and a run.

You learn a lot about yourself over time, especially during the harder spots. You know the big 'R' word everyone likes to throw around these days: resilience? Well, it's earned, baby. You're not born with it. No one's coming to save the day for you. Go figure out how to be your own bloody hero!

About the Author

Jennifer St John is creatively driven in life. Her love for art and design flourished during her school years and lead to a Design education in post-secondary. She transitioned into the Film and Television industry securing internships under the art and Producing umbrellas. Producing won and a few years later, she became co-owner of Cache Film and Television in Toronto. After several successful projects, parenthood entered the picture and pulled her into the next phase of life. Juggling motherhood and becoming a socially minded business owner became the new goal. After several years in development, Jennifer launched her new company in 2020. 'Marnie and Michael' is an artisan shop meets mental health initiative. Handmade leather products are locally produced with a percentage of profits going towards supporting family members who have a loved one with mental health challenges. Jennifer lives with her husband and two children in Penetanguishene, Ontario, Canada.

Connect With Jennifer St. John:

Website: www.marnieandmichael.com
Instagram: marnieandmichael

CHAPTER EIGHT

Rising From the Ashes

By Shane Gitmed

My name is Shane, and I am happy you are here reading about my mompreneur journey as a single mom. I have been told many times that I am the definition of a serial entrepreneur. I love anything business related and love launching all types of businesses which I enjoy and am passionate about. I own multiple businesses and work on a family business with my parents. Over the years, I realized that, along with my complex personality, I enjoy working and trying new things. This explains why I am involved in different types of businesses and working on other projects I can't wait to launch. Once I figured out a way to successfully earn income from home in 2012, I could not stop researching and trying new ways to make a living with a flexible schedule.

The current businesses I am focusing on are my travel business as a certified travel agent and my parents' business, Alkatech Water Ionizer. I am the type of person who loves to learn as much as I can, and if it is something I can make profitable, then I am all for it. There are a lot of benefits to having a travel business, one of which is getting great discounts for your own travel. You learn more ways to find great deals through the various companies, and I enjoy helping others save money.

As a parent, you want to be able to give your child fun trips and various experiences, so I am so happy I can do it without overpaying. I am a retired extreme couponer and still score great deals on everything I need to buy for my family. During my extreme couponer days, I would teach my friends and anyone who inquired on how to coupon. I even made a PowerPoint presentation at one point, so I could send it to whoever wanted to learn. I have always loved being as helpful as possible to those around me, so this business does not feel like a job to me when I work with my clients. My goal is to make their vacation planning as stress-free as possible. I truly believe it is important to find out what makes you excited and passionate when starting a business. It will never feel like a job if it is something you genuinely enjoy doing.

My parents' business, which I am actively a part of and helping grow, has changed my life. I rave about it so much because I have experienced first-hand the benefits of alkaline water. Just like the food you eat, the quality of the water you drink is also very important for your health. This business came to life because our mission is to educate as many people as possible about the amazing benefits of alkaline water and how it is the cleanest and most cost-saving water option for your family. One of my favorite things about it is how much you are helping the environment by not buying plastic water bottles and always having access to clean water at home. I love that our machines have multiple functions, too. You can select a different pH level for your water, and it could be used as face wash, disinfectant, and an effective way to wash all your fruits and vegetables. It is the only water we drink and cook with in our home, and I love knowing that I am reducing the exposure of acidic water you will find from major retailers. We have so many happy clients and have expanded greatly since it was launched.

I was born in the Bay Area and raised in Northern California. I've lived here for most of my life until I moved away shortly after high school. I'd never thought I would live anywhere outside of California. I will always be a California girl at heart, but it was a great adventure to have had the opportunity to travel and live in different parts of the country. For many years, I was a military spouse, and I got to live in Texas and Georgia. I was married to someone I had been with since high school, and we decided to get married around the same time he started his military career. The challenges I faced as a military wife were always being away from family and friends, having to start over and adjust every time you have to move. You eventually get used to it, and thanks to technology, the distance was not as bad. Luckily, at each duty station, I met amazing people who have become some of my best friends. One of them is also a business owner and owns a very successful Mexican restaurant in Texas called Preferida De Monterrey. I look back and remember the times we would talk about our goals and dreams before we had our kids. Now our hard work has paid off, and we get to enjoy what we have built for our families.

I was blessed to become a mom in a state that I love so dearly, Georgia. I found out I was pregnant in 2016 and had my son in the summer of 2017. It was a very exciting time for our family because we had a lot of big but great changes coming up. My son's father was making a career leap, and we were getting ready to move back home to California. It felt like the perfect time to expand our family so we could enjoy time with our loved ones while raising the baby. In military life, it is extremely rare to be able to be active duty while living in your home state, so it was an opportunity we had to take.

I became a mompreneur shortly after I found out I was pregnant. I knew that day that I wanted to be as present as possible while raising my son, so I had to figure out ways to continue earning a living from home. As a military spouse, you get used to your significant other being gone a lot, whether it is for a deployment, training exercise, or short-term missions. I was accustomed to being the one to stay behind and take care of everything back at home. This role taught me so much and has definitely benefited me in the world of business. I have been working remotely since 2012 and gained experience from multiple companies over the years until I went fully independent. Another reason I continued to maintain a remote career is so I could take my business everywhere I needed to move to. That flexibility was rare and hard to find, but I always somehow got lucky with finding great opportunities which brought a lot of value into my life.

The first business I started was providing business management and marketing services to small business owners. It was the best feeling to become my own boss again and made me really excited for what was to come and to apply my business administration degree and marketing experience. Every day, I did my research on how to scale my business and learned about new technology tools. I was blessed to have seen great results and got to work with wonderful clients. This new chapter was both exciting and overwhelming as I was also newly pregnant. Luckily, I had a smooth pregnancy, so it was more about just trying to prepare as much as possible. Over time, I was getting so many clients and I wanted to continue to expand, so I decided to create a marketing agency that provided even more services beyond my expertise. This move was pivotal for me because I was able to continue to grow my business throughout my pregnancy and while being a new mom. I am so thankful to have an amazing team I can rely on through the highs and lows. If it were not for them, I would not have been able to explore the other business ideas I had and launch them.

The motto, "Work smarter not harder," was something I really wanted to apply in every way possible because I knew that by being a working mom who works remotely, I wanted to keep my schedule flexible. Back at the drawing board, I wanted to find ways to make passive income. My goal was to have multiple income streams, and I found the results I was looking for in e-commerce and other partnerships. The serial entrepreneur in me kept going down the rabbit hole, so one store turned into three. Throughout my mompreneur journey, I have come across other like-minded individuals for whom I am so grateful because it is hard to meet others in general when you work from home. From those connections, I gained business partners who have been amazing to work with, and we are always bouncing ideas off each other. It has been a pleasure to collaborate with other business owners, and there are so many projects we cannot wait to launch in the future.

The main thing that keeps me driven and passionate about the work I do is the impact I am making in people's lives. Whether they are a customer who bought a product, a client I helped grow their business, or a family I planned a trip for, I get great joy from helping people and being a problem-solver for them. I love knowing I can be of service to others with my talents and making a difference in their lives, regardless of which business they became my client in. I do plan on launching a couple of things where I get to see the people I am serving in person. As much as I have enjoyed doing most of my work online, I am excited to be more active within my community.

When I think of the adversity I faced starting from the beginning of my mompreneur journey up until this very day, I see, now more than ever, how resilient I am. I am thankful to be blessed in so many ways, but the adversity that comes with being a single mother is something I never thought would happen to me. I can say that working through and overcoming the adversities has made me an overall stronger and wiser person. Going through a divorce is never easy, especially when there are children involved and while you are trying to maintain your career. Everything you have ever known is now not the same, and you are trying to navigate how you are going to start over. Unfortunately, my family and I faced countless challenges in a very short amount of time, which caused so much more stress and grief that it took a toll on us. The biggest tragedy was when my father-in-law unexpectedly passed away three days before my son was born. We were grieving a loss but also had a bundle of joy that was the light of our lives. To honor him, I made his name my son's middle name, Paul. It was on that day that life as I knew it was never going to be the same.

My whole mission for gaining success in my businesses was for my family because I so badly wanted to gain financial freedom and be able to be fully present for my son. When my ex-husband and I separated, my whole world was shattered. This was someone with whom I'd spent 10 years of my life and intended on having a growing family with. For a long time, it felt like my worst nightmare that I could not believe was real. I was terrified of being a new mom, not to mention a single one due to the lack of support I would have. I could not wrap my head around what was going to be my new reality: single mom to a child under two years old, business owner, dog mom to two, and only knowing a handful of people in the city I live in because my family and friends lived two hours away. I have attempted multiple times to try and relocate so we could be closer to them, but it has not been in the cards. I suffer from anxiety which was at its worst after my son was born. I struggled with trying to figure out how I was going to manage everything by myself, but I knew that giving up was not an option and that I had to make it work for my family. I was so afraid to fail because I had so much pressure on me, but I did whatever it took so we could continue to survive.

As someone who is an advocate for mental health, I was concerned that the effects of the string of tragedies that were happening in my life would affect my parenting. The feelings of anxiety and depression would come and go, so I made sure to get back into therapy and practice a lot of self-care. I have always been an independent and self-reliant person, but the love and support I got whenever I needed it truly saved me. I grew up with a single mom, and I saw the struggles she had to face, so I was not okay with the fact that it felt like history was repeating itself. By living and witnessing first-hand how hard it is to take care of a family on your own, I just kept praying for guidance.

There was a time when I had to take some time to step back and process what I was going through. I had to focus on my mental health and work on healing, so I did need to ask for help from my peers so my businesses would continue to run smoothly. For once, I put myself first so I could be the best version of myself for my family. Part of taking care of myself is staying on top of my health. To top it off, I was facing a cancer scare. I had been going to specialists over the years and was not able to get answers I needed. Around the time my marriage was splitting up, my symptoms were getting worse. I had to have procedures done to check for signs of cancer, and luckily, I was in the clear. I ended up addressing my health concerns with alternative medicine, and it changed my life. I finally got the answers I was looking for and got the relief I needed to start feeling better. I still use alternative medicine methods, and it has been a game changer for me. I wanted to look and feel my best so I could deliver in my businesses, so I had to think outside of the box.

I like to look at life in seasons. When I was in the thick of all the changes in my life, I told myself that this next chapter was going to be my phoenix season. In mythology, there is bird called a phoenix which rises from the ashes and is born again. I wanted to view this new life of mine as the birth of the new me and rising from the ashes of my old life. That symbolism means a lot to me and whenever I need motivation, I remember what I vowed to myself. I knew that I needed a sense of community because it can get lonely as a single parent, so I chose to be active at my church again. It was the best decision I could have ever made to help me feel grounded as a person and I was happy to have made some friends through the groups I joined. My faith is what has gotten me this far and I loved that our support system in the area was growing. I felt a sense of relief and peace, which helped me get stronger as a person and as a businesswoman.

There is no definite amount of time for how long it takes to adapt to parenthood, and it constantly feels like you are learning and adjusting to something new. It is a work in progress, and I will always allow myself the time I need to grow. Regardless of how long it took and the things I had to overcome, I stayed focused on my goal and wanting to make my son proud. One day, I want to be able to share my trials and tribulations with him to show that you can overcome anything. There were people who underestimated me, and it only made me more driven to prove them wrong that I could do this and succeed. One of the things I am thankful for is my ability to not let anything get in my way and power through it. Military life taught me how to jump through hurdles and always deal with the unexpected.

Other than my church community, I've implemented a healthier lifestyle. I love all the benefits of juicing, so I regularly make my own fresh juice at home. I also started to take fitness classes at a local family club which helped me tremendously to be in a better head space overall. I made more of an effort to see our family and friends out of town. That quality time was amazing for my son so he could get to know them more. It also helped me to get out of town and be more involved in the family business.

If there is one major lesson I learned during my journey, it is how important your mindset is. If you stay in the negative, you must realize you are blocking your own abundance from happening. The more positivity you put into the world, the better the things will attract. We are all human and have our bad days, but you do not have to stay stuck in them. Just like in business, you are going to face rough patches, but you have to stay resilient and not allow anything to get in your way. I had to keep a brave face and be strong on my weakest days. You have to keep showing up for yourself and for your business. Some things are blessings in disguise. Even if you do not see it now, it will come to light.

This chapter of my life made me a stronger woman, and I am thankful for the lessons I learned. I will continue to take a chance on things because you never know where it will lead. I like to keep an open mind, and more often than not, something will surprise me. It keeps me on my toes like I feel about the different businesses I own. One day, my son will be old enough to see and understand the career that I built was all for him. Being a single parent can be overwhelming, and you will need to make sacrifices, but if you stay true to your purpose, then everything will have been worth it.

About the Author

Shane Gitmed is a serial entrepreneur, co-author, speaker, and podcast host. Her multi-passionate spirit has gotten her into various types of businesses and she continues to grow and launch her ideas. Her latest launch as of the summer of 2020 is her podcast, Carpe Diem Living. This show is special to her because the topic is about holistic/functional medicine and natural healing. Every week you get to learn from experts in the field and inspiring stories from those who were able to heal this way like Shane did. She currently resides in California with her son and two dogs.

CHAPTER NINE

Your Past Does Not Define Your Present

By Irina Rosu Dickie

As I sit in my sunny and airy study looking out the window, filling my mind with the multicolored bougainvillea adorning my garden and the sides of the empty streets, I listen to the sound of brazen, concert-like birds, a beautiful noise that is not the norm even in a suburb, in a busy city like Dubai.

I am doing some breathing exercises and meditation before starting a coaching session with a client who is a Senior Partner in a major law firm. In front of me, I have his psychometric report which I've finished interpreting, and it is ready for feedback and incorporating into our session to dig deeper and further and help him in ways he may not have envisioned.

I am an Executive Coach and Business Psychologist. Right now, organization management and business entrepreneurs all face issues with isolation, managing a remote work force while they are in isolation them-selves, building relationships with clients virtually, staff burnout and how to motivate them, and a reduction in revenue which demands the need to look at operating differently. Moms who are entrepreneurs, often single moms who put all their sweat and resources into build-ing a business, are now facing a new and unknown en-emy which can decimate their earnings and life's work. However, there is always hope, and this is where I come in.

The COVID-19 crisis has imprisoned everyone. At the time of writing, I will be able to get a permit to go to the supermarket again in three days. While the comfort and luxuries I have now do not compare, the feelings of helplessness and the lack of freedom do take me back to the times as a child growing up in communist Roma-nia in a very remote village with no running water. The nearest bus station was an hour's walk through mud and murky roads. I used to wake up at 3:00 am to catch the bus and be at the market on time to sell the cheese my mom had made from our cows. Starting out very early in the morning would allow me to catch a spot and join the queue of hundreds of people to buy two loaves of bread. For extra loaves, I needed to repeat the queue again as only two loaves were allowed per person.

Other people used to leave their shoes and an empty bag on the floor to reserve their spot in the queue. I learnt to do the same so I could save my place in the queue for oil and sugar at the same time and catch the bus back to make it to school.

I also had the monthly ration coupons to get the half-liter of cooking oil and sugar per household member. When that ran out, we had nothing to cook with. Everything in our home was rationed.

Presently, seeing people in supermarkets grabbing everything they can to stock up during the lockdown made me think of how excited we were as children during the fall of communism when we could buy whatever we wanted and fill up as many trolleys as we wanted! I remember the day when we could buy oranges without queuing and without rations, not only at Christmas as we used to, but anytime! I also remember how quickly I lost my excitement, my innocence and the hope of a better fate for my family and country when I and many people realized that food on the shelves didn't mean food on our table. Capitalism had its own darkness. This is the same capitalism that many children around the world are experiencing now in the times of COVID-19 when many governments are doing nothing to support them and many are going to sleep hungry.

Although I was the youngest of seven siblings and a child myself, my mom trusted only me to run her errands and, most importantly, to sell her small produce. I was her little reliable and responsible helper who had to behave like an adult. I had built my own client base, and they used to wait for me at the same time during certain days of the week. I am not sure whether they were buying from me because our product was better than others or because of the pity to see a child so young do the job of an adult. I was grateful, nonetheless, and tried to retain their loyalty.

The bus journey was an hour each way, and I needed to return to school. With 10 to 15 kgs of cheese I used to carry on my back, I remember stopping and changing hands as it felt like they were breaking. My husband often now laughs at the strength of my grip, that it's stronger than his!

The land my grandparents owned had been taken away from them during the Communist regime. Our family even owned a forest, but both my grandfather and father were political prisoners for refusing to sign away the family land out of love for the system. They took it anyway! As a result, our family was doomed to poverty and we were raising livestock and working the land for the state while our family starved. The cheese I sold was our percentage we were allowed to keep for our own consumption, but we couldn't afford to eat it.

This was the start of my entrepreneurial journey at a very young age. As my parents did not have an income, I had to find ways to make my own. I couldn't say how this came about. I did not have any role models. It was just survival.

I used to pick medicinal plants in the spring. I organized a group of children to pick cherries during the summer and negotiate the rates on their behalf. We worked on apples and corn crops during the autumn. The winters were the worst. There was five months of desperation and worry for the next day. The bread would go stale and rock hard, and my mom would put it on the steam in a pot to make it edible for as long as possible. The roads would be blocked with snow and we were unable to go and buy essentials.

The communists did not care about the forgotten villages, and it would take weeks for the snow to be removed, only to be blocked again by a blizzard. We would walk 22 km through the high snow, off road, digging out of it as we fell, to buy bread in the only village that had a bakery. On the way back, my sister and I would carry the bags on our backs.

Wolves would often venture out, always near the same Jewish cemetery, which terrified me as a child with ghost stories of all sorts. I carried matches and old newspapers to burn. Once, I even had to burn my clothes to chase them away. The trip would always be longer as we had to wait in several queues for hours to buy the rations. Getting up at 3:00 am and catching the bus at 4:00 am in the spring, summer, or autumn, and walking to the next village in the winters when the roads were blocked allowed me enough time to get back and go to school.

Most often, I chose to walk instead, saving the bus fare to buy books. Those books and my love of studies were my escape. I loved reading, and I loved studying! Our two-year-old toddler now seems to have inherited my love of books, and at times, I joke with my husband that our next house will have to have a library. The feel of books on your fingers can never be matched by a Kindle! I used to keep my books under the bed or stash them under the mattress and take them out at night, hiding behind the window curtains with a gas lamp on the window sill or simply the full moon light and read until 4 am. My father found me once, and he bought me a rechargeable torch. My mom would just tear the pages from the books to stop me from wasting my nights on reading. Once, when she took away one of my favorite books, I was so upset and cried so much that I passed out.

With the fall of the communism, however, all the qualified teachers, save one, left the village to return to the urban areas. The regime forcibly assigned them in remote areas. They were replaced by high school graduates who were called substitutes. I think that hit me more than anything at the time. I still remember the pain and desperation for my lost future.

I started to study on my own, and I became really good at it, so good that I passed my exams and was admitted into one of the best high schools in the county. My parents couldn't support me through it, so I worked for several local magazines and spent all my summers working as a waitress and washing dishes at the Black Sea Coast hotels.

I had nightmares for years that I was sleeping in the streets. It only stopped several years ago when I trained as a coach and dealt with it. I was moving from place to place almost every month as I struggled to pay for accommodation. I commuted for my final baccalaureate exams, and I remember walking into the exams exhausted from the hours-long trip that I would have to repeat every day for the whole week. I don't know how I achieved top results in most of the subjects. It feels surreal now when I look back as all I can remember is that exhaustion which made me nauseous.

As soon as I graduated, I packed one small, brown cloth bag which I had bought cheaply from a kiosk, and I left for the airport. I didn't look back when my mom collapsed to her knees crying that she might never see me again. I had the equivalent of 10 dollars in Romanian leu in my pocket, which we borrowed from my aunt. I needed it for my bus and train fare and was left with nothing when I boarded the aircraft. No one that we knew had ever left the country. Getting visas and working abroad legally was still a dream for the majority when the Romanian passport was worth nothing.

I didn't see or speak to my family for two years. I wrote letters which took months to deliver. My parents didn't have a phone. That was the hardest part I had to deal with. I was so young and I missed them so much that I cried myself to sleep reading their letters over and over again. Now, my elderly parents are in isolation, and though we can speak every day and I see them on VOIP, I don't know when I'll see them again as we are thousands of miles apart and both countries are in lockdown. Unlike back then, time is even more precious now.

After I joined one of the best international airlines as a cabin crew member, I went to visit my parents and treated them to everything they ever dreamt of. I set up a monthly allowance in addition to improving their life in every respect.

Life as a stewardess was a dream. We would spend a week in St Tropez, three days in Athens, five days in Thailand, three days in Paris, Rome, Jakarta, Singapore, Brisbane, Sydney, Colombo to name just a few. We met celebrities and joined the film festivals and concert after-parties.

The freedom provided by this job, along with my entrepreneurial skills I acquired as a child, made me want to have financial freedom by the time I was 40. When I got my first paycheck, I started planning for my financial freedom. The fear of poverty was so deeply ingrained that all the five-star hotels I was staying in and the lifestyle I suddenly had felt like a daydream from which I could wake up at any time.

As Romania was very cheap at the time, and I foresaw the entry into the European Union, not because of economic strength but because of its geographical position, I used my first savings to buy an apartment in the town near my parents which was just US$6000. Instead of spending my holidays as every young girl who never had a childhood would have wanted to, making up for all the fun I never had, I spent them renovating the apartment and learning about real estate and building structures. Three years later, I sold it for $41,000.

The same year, I took a loan to supplement my savings, and I bought an apartment in the center of Bucharest overlooking the Place of the Parliament, which already had a tenant paying €500 a month, five times the minimum salary per economy. That apartment also went up five times in price in the course of a few years when

Romania's economy started to drastically improve, mainly due to its joining the EU.

My financial education took precedence for a while, and I bought and read all the books on fundamentals of investing and momentum trading that I could possibly buy. (I was a loyal visitor of different libraries around the world, especially in Waterstones in Portugal Street in London near the university where I started studying.) I set up an online margin account in the UK, but it was offshore based. This became a hobby which paid off very well.

In my job, I had so many days off and tickets to travel anywhere I wanted on the spur of the moment, I applied for London School of Economics External Program. I travelled to London on all my days off and completed my degree. As soon as it was completed, I went for a Masters in Organisational Psychology in London. By then, I was in a leadership role and also a trainer at the airline. Education enabled a quick move through the ranks, and I was managing 150 cabin managers, doing leadership coaching and managing all their performance. Eventually, I took a managerial position as a secondment where I managed 2000 new cabin crew. With the Masters in Organizational Psychology, I qualified as Psychometric Test User (formerly Level A and B) and got certified in several personality instruments. What really triggered my extensive training as a coach, which later became my own business, with a reputed university like Ashridge Executive Education, was when I faced an organizational unjust act within the airline that I worked for.

The airline was and still is one of the best companies to work for, and I loved it and gave my loyalty to it, but like every entity, it is the people or that one person you end up working for who makes the difference. The treatment from that one person was so unjust, I became paralyzed for years, unable to move ahead in my career, being extremely afraid of any type of visibility. The shame and the cruelty, the unfairness of the outcome (which I couldn't prove, nor did I try), hit me so hard that I lost complete sight of where I had come from, the far more difficult and risky journey that I had travelled. One of my strengths as a coach now is helping people get out of being stuck, of feelings of doubt and often shame caused by a past incident or identifying the roots, which sometimes we are not even aware of.

I do not take anything as a coincidence. It was meant to happen when it did. I was trained as a performance and leadership coach. I did so much training in-house and externally, and I was great at helping other people. They got results. They changed, and their careers took off every day. Their in-house reviews on how I helped them were getting brighter and brighter every day while I was sinking into a darker and darker place which sucked my energy and left me stuck in the same place, professionally and emotionally. You shouldn't coach without having a strong support in place from a coaching supervisor, yet this support does not really exist in most organizations where the management is involved in coaching.

I was my own worst enemy. During every assessment center and promotional interview I was going for, I felt like someone was watching me and talking about me in a negative way as when it happened before, even if this was years ago.

Soon after, I was diagnosed with endometriosis. My body's way of coping with the negative emotions started to show. Our gut is where the second brain resides, where our instinct speaks to us and channels all the communication energy. My liver took a hit, too, and I had adenomas with precancerous cells.

One day, while I was at a Business Psychology lecture in London, I made a friend who was an Executive Coach and studied at Ashridge Business School. She coached me using a unique depth I'd never experienced before. The years of heaviness, the drain of energy that my subconscious was consuming to survive, lifted and allowed me to "see" and allowed my self to be seen for the very first time in years. Of course, that was only a start since those issues had been with me for so long! The real transformation happened later, during my coaching course and journey.

As I am writing now, my last scan was six months ago, and CA 125 for endometriosis and liver, an illness said to have no cure, was clear. So is the constant heaviness I knew not where it was coming from.

I knew that one person does not define a great organization that I loved, but at that point, my desire to leave sprouted in my subconscious as a seed which kept growing without my knowledge.

While travelling with my job, I met CEOs of different companies around the world, business entrepreneurs, managers whom I coached on every possible organizational and personal issue.

I started my coaching practice alongside my work, but after I delivered my baby, based on the maternity law of the company, I had to go back to work after four months. I hired a nanny well before going back to work, to train her to look after him. One night, we found she had brought strange men in our house while we were there. When we called security, we found out that this was a regular occurrence. I took my son, who was two months old at the time, to check for signs of abuse. That was the point when I decided to set up my own business and look after my own child.

I started working on my website and doing my last client case studies which I had to send to the University. Marketing myself and having all the clients promote me through testimonials and word of mouth became paramount for the organic growth I was looking for.

Soon after, my son was diagnosed with hip dysplasia. He was nine months old, and that was a very late diagnosis. This would normally need to be diagnosed at six weeks for the treatment to be successful. The same day I found out he had the condition, they put him in a brace for 23 hours a day until he was 2 years old. We had no guarantee it would work. He also had to wear a helmet for 23 hours a day for a flat spot on his head at the same time.

Below is an excerpt of the diary I kept as a coping mechanism. This diary helped me vent my emotions, helped me through my self-coaching, and gave me strength to go on. I set it up as an email account for my son and wrote him an email every day. One day, when he is old enough, he will get the password.

16 October 2018

"Today, my life turned upside when the doctor told me you have hip dysplasia. I don't even know what this is or means. He started to measure and mark your shoulder harness for a brace he immobilised you with. You looked at me and the doctor with your big grey eyes asking why you were immobilised when you wanted to roll on the medical table.

I kept my tears from rolling and smiled at you to encourage you that it was all okay, but you felt my energy and pain and started crying.

I went numb and walked you back to the car where I put you in the car seat like I was in sleepwalking, worried that you might not fit in it, but you did.

At home, your father left his work to come and see you. You were on the sofa with your legs up like a small bee, unable to turn because of the brace, and I saw your father's eyes clouding but he smiled broadly to encourage the both of us.

I had to change your nappy, but my hands were shaking. I didn't know how to remove your brace and put it back on. My brain didn't register anything the doctor had told us.

Out of the brace, you rolled onto your back and started rolling all over the mat. You looked at me with your big eyes imploring me not to put you back in the brace. Your beautiful face and grey eyes were saying: "Look, Mummy, I can do all this. Do not put me back in the brace!"

With this look, you break my heart 10 times a day.

We went to the playground and you saw the other babies crawling and moving to get their toys. You turned and wanted to follow them, but you fell on your side with your legs immobilised by the brace and you started crying. My heart never stops shattering in pieces...

When we go to the hospital, I look at other babies with bigger problems than yours, and I try to be grateful, but I still feel a constant heartache and wonder where you find your strength to smile every day, that smile which makes my life worth living."

It set me back. For a coach who needed all her internal resources to help others, I felt void and unable even to carry on with my day-to-day life. This helplessness and desperation lasted a couple of weeks while I hid myself in the shower and cried and cried. Then, I remembered who I am and the strength I have, so I coached myself out of it and tried to be grateful that we were treating his legs and avoided thinking about what the doctor had said in his office: "He might never walk". That "might" was a lot more improbable than the definitive diagnosis I was given and won over it.

I printed out and placed on my fridge a statement that always helped me:

"Be careful about your self-talk. It's a conversation with the Universe"

Every time my mind tried to slip into negativity, I used Transactional Analysis, which I often use with my clients, to attend to myself and find love for myself through the internal Nurturing Parent. With that, I could have the energy and resources to be there for my son and family and to look after my clients and business.

I created a vision board with positive photos and custom-written statements (describing exactly my own situation and not just broad statements). I looked at it and visualized it every morning and night: my son healthy, running on a playground. In the mornings, I would stay with my son in the garden and while he looked through his books and toys. I would meditate for 15 minutes and clear my mind and regain energy before I started coaching a client.

My baby could not sleep in his brace, and the helmet made him soaking wet for the first few weeks. I woke up every 45 minutes to an hour to turn him to the other side and make him comfortable. The helmet was also very dangerous for overheating if he had fever. This was one year of absolutely no sleep. While it was so hard, I had reduced the numbers of clients per week so I could attend to myself, but I carried on working on my business.

I took time every day to mourn the loss of my old life where I could sleep, be free, have a highly paid job which took me around the globe, and welcome the new life with the love of my life in it, with that baby who loved me more than anything in his life and with that medical problem I had no control of. Everyone needs to mourn on a regular basis, as life keeps taking us into the next stage and the past remains behind. Mourning helps with closure and accepting what's coming next with excitement rather than regret, allowing new energy to come in and the old negative one to go out ("Mourning and Melancholia", Freud).

I wrote notes with specific things I mourned for and tore them up at the end of it, leaving only the ones for my new life.

To self-coach, I used the questions like the ones below and wrote down the answers several times every day in the form of a diary:

- When did I start feeling this way?

- What do I feel? What thoughts go through my mind when I think of this issue?

- What bodily sensations do I experience?

- How do I overcome this? What is the first thing I could do?

- What will happen when I face my issue without fear?

- What will change in my thoughts, feelings, behavior, when I do that?

- What will be different when I am out of this impasse? What steps can I take (emotional, practical) to get closer to that?

I remember coaching other new mompreneurs who were dealing with guilt and role conflict, and one whose child had an accident while she was working. As a coach who employs relational coaching, I was healing myself at the same time as healing her, and I only realized that when my coaching supervisor pointed it out.

I wished I had known of coaching a long time ago in my career and paid for a coach to free this energy which built in my subconscious, the stuckness which prevented me from going ahead in my life and career, that energy which ate away at me and left me without motivation or strength to go on. From the child who did not believe in convention, who never felt fear of anything and went ahead despite all the obstacles, I became, for many years, someone without any belief in myself, someone who constantly looked over her shoulder and wondered if the management in the room whispered about how incompetent I was.

When I started, and even now occasionally, I do pro bono work for different reasons (paying it forward, personal development, etc.). I would recommend to anyone who struggles and doesn't even know what the problems are to find a good coach with whom they feel very comfortable and explore it! Invest in yourself first, then you will have all the resources to look after your business and your career, everything and everyone else in your life. You may fall in desperation, lose everything you worked for or have to start again.

Ask the Universe for help, and it will come to you! What is important is that your eyes are open to see the shapes it may come as. Persist, no matter how many times you fall on your knees.

Remember this: Every material thing in your life is dispensable; the only one who is not is you!! YOU are the only world that matters!

About the Author

Irina Rosu Dickie, MSc, MABP has engaged in coaching and mentoring throughout her career. She also has extensive experience in training and development, leadership and selection and assessment.

Although based in Dubai, Irina regularly travels worldwide and has a broad exposure to Middle Eastern and international cultures. Her passion and talents are in helping people develop holistically across areas that transcend their professional life.

Her coaching style draws on a variety of psychological models to enable the transformation from within.

Irina holds an Executive Coaching Certification from Ashridge Executive Education and a MSc in Organisational Psychology from Birkbeck College, London.

Her academic studies, professional and coaching experience have provided an in-depth knowledge of individual and group behaviour and solidified her understanding of organisational change and development. In addition, she is professional member of the Association for Business Psychology and associate member of Society of Industrial and Organisational Psychology, she is certified as a Psychometric Test User by the British Psychological Society and is a specialist in the use of a number of instruments.

Irina has coached clients from a variety of industries: Aviation, Law, Sales, HR and Recruitment, Finance, Entrepreneurs and Gig Workers.

She is qualified and experienced to help in a broad range of organisational and business aspects however she places a deeper focus on helping entrepreneurs to remove self-doubt and expand their business, Organizational Justice, Remote Work Leadership, Work and Well Being, Organisational Change and the changing future of work and business and helping management, professionals and entrepreneurs "partner" with Artificial Intelligence for enhanced performance and productivity and for selection and assessment.

Connect with Irina Rosu-Dickie:

Website: https://www.portalcoachingexec.com/

Facebook:
www.facebook.com/Portalcoachingandconsulting

Linkedin: https://www.linkedin.com/in/irina-rosu-dickie-msc-mabp-4893b546/

CHAPTER TEN

Turning Your Brilliant Ideas Into Your Brilliant Life

By Laurel Bloomfield

My entrepreneurial lessons started early in life. I started my first business when I was nine years old to help with my struggling family's finances. I actually did pretty darn good for a nine-year-old. From that young age, I learned there is nothing greater than a trial in life to provide the keys to success. If only one would see them that way, there is great profit to be had in overcoming obstacles. Looking back, I can pinpoint one event which pivoted my life path very early on, brought so many things into a profoundly clear perspective for me, and really set me up for a very successful life.

It was a crisp spring morning. We had boarded the ski bus at 5:00 AM and headed for the mountain. Our team skied this same small ski resort a couple of times a week for ski practice, so I knew this hill like the back of my hand. I loved these early mornings!

I hopped on a lift with my two friends, "the Jennys". At the top, we took the catwalk over to one of our favorite runs to start the day. Blonde Jenny was in front with Brunette Jenny in back, singing I Like Big Butts, Ice, Ice Baby, and a compilation of many other silly songs of the day, giggling the whole way as 15-year-old girls do. The sun was so bright, the run perfectly groomed. We were the first ones there. I can still remember the glistening rainbows reflecting off the snow so brightly. We lined up, smirked at each other, and I took off like a shot, skis pointed straight down the hill, calling back, "See you at the bottom! Loser buys the hot chocolate!" Still giggling and singing, a feeling of pure freedom and joy washed over me. Little did we know that, in less than 30 seconds, I would have an accident which would nearly kill me.

Ten hours later, I was still in emergency surgery where the medical team was struggling to stop the internal bleeding. My parents had barely made it over the mountain to the hospital to give me a kiss as they wheeled me in to surgery. They told me many years later that they almost didn't make it over the mountain to get to me. The highway closed right behind them due to a bad snowstorm, and the highway patrol had reluctantly let them through. Just a few minutes into surgery, one of my surgeons came back out to brief them, saying, "If we can't stop the bleeding in five minutes, we will need to Life Flight her to Reno where there is a vascular surgeon waiting to amputate her leg, but it's a 17.5 minute flight.

We are not sure if she will survive the flight. She has lost too much blood already." As a parent now, I can imagine the fear my parents were experiencing during those moments and hours they waited.

Lying on the operating table, I couldn't remember how I got there. As I opened my eyes and looked around, I could see a blue sheet in front of my face, bright lights, and white walls. I rolled my eyes back, looked up and smiled at the anesthesiologist sitting by my head as I asked, "Why are there no colors in this room?" He visibly jumped, took my face in his hands with tears in his eyes and whispered, "Hi there, sweet girl. I am so glad you are here. I'm going to put you back to sleep now and everything is going to be okay." As my eyes began to close again, I saw him looking up over the blue sheet, and I heard him say "Guys, she's back!" A roar of cheers erupted from my medical team. Anytime life gets hard for me, I put myself back in that moment, and it's easy for me to be grateful for another day to take a shot at this great adventure called life.

I went into that day, March 2, 1995, as a silly, happy teenage girl and came out with a totally different life. It took a while to adjust to my new perspective, but that day really gave me the gift of "knowing" once experienced, you can never go back. I received the gift of knowing there is more: more to life, more after this life, and more for me to do in this life I am so grateful for. Because of that moment, I always have this little reminder that I really am capable of anything and there is nothing to fear.

It took a year for me to be able to walk again. I had a world-class medical team that got me there, and I learned so much from them. I was literally surrounded by a medical team who quickly became my heroes. The surgeon who happened to be on call the day of my accident traveled around the world to busy ski resort town hospitals, chasing these kinds of cases. He was world-renowned for compartment syndrome and had saved several limbs and lives already that year, while most of his colleagues called themselves "lucky" if they were able to see one case like mine in their lifetime. He just happened to be in the Truckee hospital that day. My follow-up surgeon was the winningest gold medalist of all time at the time, Eric Heiden, and my physical therapist's son was an Olympic skier, too. I constantly felt so much gratitude to have the opportunity to be surrounded by their greatness.

One afternoon, during a very painful physical therapy session, I was crying and discouraged. I was a long way from walking again, and it felt like I would probably never ski again. I asked my doctor, "Are you ever going to say I will be able to ski again?" He replied, "As soon as I give you the okay to walk, I expect you to ski the very next day! Don't put any time in between or you will never ski again." What a great parallel to entrepreneurship. Every time I have "failed", I try to put as little space between said failure and my next "try" as possible. If you do, the fear may win and take you out of the game.

Now, 20-something years later, I can look back on the all the trials of my life and see exactly how they led me to this exact moment, exactly where I am supposed to be, and I wouldn't change a thing.

I started my first "grown-up" business during my last year of college, in the animal health industry. Today, I am a mom and a wife, married to a fifth-generation cattle rancher. For the past 15 years, we have built several businesses together and have been able to really push and support each other in each of our own ventures, too. I have taken so many tries at the things I want out of life and business, and let me tell you I have fallen flat on my face more times than I can count, but I have always gotten right back up and hopped back on the horse (or skis, literally 😊).

I had just transitioned from college to owning my own business when I met and married my fellow entrepreneur husband. We are both patented inventors, and I have been able to take those experiences building those ideas into businesses and help many others launch their big ideas into actual revenue generating businesses; from navigating the patent process to product creation, manufacturing and scaling into major distribution. Some of my projects include Pocket Innerwear®, Pro ReLeaf ™, The Puke Bucket® 😊, Wack Rack™, Revel Wear ™, and several others. I am so fortunate now to be able to work on so many creative projects with other inventors and help them turn their business goals into reality. It has been a fun and wild ride, and I really feel like it's just the beginning.

I was 25 when we got married, and I had already accomplished so much that I was totally ready and content to be marrying my dream guy, living out in the middle of nowhere and just raising cows and babies. We started trying for those babies right away, but what I had naively thought would take a couple months became a seven-year journey through my own version of Hell. Those were seven years of trying and failing, month after month of negative drug store pregnancy tests, then several positives turned into devastating losses, our entire life savings spent on fertility treatments, and obstacle after obstacle thrown in our path.

When I was 32, we finally adopted our miracle baby at birth. The moment I witnessed his first breath, everything was right in my world. It all made total sense, and I would relive those seven years of pain a million times if it meant I could just have one minute of loving him. After seven years of Hell, the moment he was born, I experienced Heaven on Earth.

I have been so fortunate to have had a wonderfully successful marriage (the most important partnership in my life). We have been able to use those skills we developed early on to participate in many other successful business partnerships together and with others. I can always look back on how we handled our journey through infertility as what has set us apart. It forced us to communicate deeper than a lot of newlyweds. It gave us some phenomenal team-building skills and the confidence that, no matter how many times or how painfully life knocks us down, we just keep getting back up and going for it. We know we overcame that seemingly insurmountable obstacle together and created the life we wanted. Any curveball business throws at us pales in comparison to the battle we fought to create our family.

The key takeaway from that, which has helped me most in business, is that, no matter what, you are a team. When things go wrong, and they will, when mistakes are made, and they are going to be, you absolutely cannot ever turn against each other looking for someone to blame. You have to turn towards each other looking for a solution. I cannot stress this enough. Blame is a waste of time, and the moment that becomes the culture in business, in relationships, in life, you will make it so much harder for everyone involved to find a way out of the problem at hand. All teams need to always be solution focused, never blame focused. There is no point in pointing a finger at someone ever. Period. End of story. It's that simple. The mindset of your team is your greatest asset or your greatest liability.

No matter how bad it is, there is always tomorrow. You can try again, and if you have a good partner by your side, you can accomplish anything. I got into that mindset from a very young age. I took those skills into my adult life, in my marriage, and through the hardest battle of my life so far. No matter what, no matter how hard I cried, no matter how deeply my heart was broken, I woke up the next day and mustered the courage to be grateful for another shot. It is important to allow yourself to experience the bad. Those negative emotions are always valid, but they can't stick around for long. When you are given another day, you have to make the most of it and just do that repeatedly. You will eventually reach all of your goals if you can do this one thing.

I was born as a positive, even tempered, understanding person. I count those all as gifts. I can't really take credit for that, but I have built on all those traits throughout life, and those gifts that I built up to skills have served me really well in relationships. Good relationships translate into whatever kind of success you want. Business is all about relationships.

I am turning 40 this year, and I am happy to say at this point in my life, I am not really scared of anything. I can happily walk the tightrope between success and failure for a long time. From starting a business when I was nine to a near-death experience in my teenage years to battling infertility with my husband to building several successful businesses to failing at just as many, I now have built up courage, endurance, and persistence which help me continue to reach my benchmarks for success and to always be aiming for new benchmarks.

I believe each of us has a very different path, but we can all relate to adversity. We all have faced many obstacles in life, and while those challenges are different stories, they all have parallels which connect us. We can look back at how our lives have shaped us into the people we are. I am grateful for all my struggles. Thankfully, I have been fortunate to be able to come out on the other side of those obstacles and see how everything has worked out for my good. If you haven't gotten there yet, if you are in the midst of a trial, I can 100% promise you that you will come out the other side.

I have become more patient throughout life, and each lesson in patience has served me well in the next obstacle I would inevitably face. Working for a year to be able to walk again or waiting seven years for a baby, having a business partnership blow up in a nasty way, and business failures have all been incredible exercises in patience.

If I had one nugget of advice, it would be to keep on going, stop stopping, trust yourself and trust people in general, be patient with yourself and others, choose to see the good in yourself and others, and look for those teammates in life to help you through. Finally, here's a really important piece: once you've found a good teammate, treat them as a treasure. (Okay, well, maybe that's a few nuggets of advice. 😊)

Something my husband always says, which has stuck with me, is simple but gets me through some tough times. I call it Cowboy Logic: "No matter how hard the winter, spring always comes."

About the Author

Laurel Bloomfield is a patented inventor and the founder of Revelwear Inc., Pocket Innerwear Inc., DMD Digital LLC., and Laurel Bloomfield LLC and several other companies she started, scaled and then sold. Laurel oversaw the development of various products from their initial idea to selling in major retailers. She offers her guidebooks, business building resources and her Patent Workshops at: www.laurelbloomfield.com

Her patented inventions are distributed in Target and Walgreen's and she now helps other inventors navigate the myriad steps required to see their brilliant idea become a commercial success

One of her first patents was a clothing line with specially-designed built-in pockets to safely hold insulin pumps for Type-1 diabetics. After working through the entire process of concept, prototype, final design, patent and distribution to major retailers, Laurel sold the company and turned her attention to guiding others through the complicated process via her companies DMD Digital and Laurel Bloomfield LLC. She recently had the opportunity to buy back into the clothing company which will be relaunched as RevelWear later this year.

Laurel could be described as the All-American Girl-Next-Door. Married to a 5th generation Cattle Rancher, she and her husband live in the middle of nowhere, enjoying being surrounded by solitude and nature while they raise their son and brood of animals.

A passionate entrepreneur since her childhood, Laurel's love of helping others succeed has made her a highly-sought after speaker, mentor and consultant.

CHAPTER ELEVEN

Rising Up

A Story of Learning to Move Forward. Always Forward.

By Katie Larsen

Waves were crashing on the beach just beyond our little hotel room patio, and the sun was sinking into the ocean. We were tired and happy and thrilled to be exactly where we were. I still look back on that evening we sat in San Diego making a couple of phone calls, talking about the progress we had made, and sitting in moments of quiet just listening to the surf. If I could bottle contentment, satisfaction, and entrepreneurial thrill, I would go back to that evening with a mason jar to do it (cue next business brainstorm). Laurel and I sat there and shared in the elation of success and progress. We were in meetings with all the right players. We called our people in Australia to report the news of the day. We had a key meeting with Medtronic and Tandem Diabetes. Everything was in place to make our next move in the medical device industry. Then, we dined on the beach. There is little more I could have asked for.

If I'm being honest, there were many moments like this along the way. There was one hilarious and wild evening spent at a Hollywood movie opening party. The theme was masquerade, and we bounced around that scene a little awkwardly, but happy to have another opportunity to learn and grow. We walked the streets of Chicago after meeting with Walgreens. We stayed in the Disneyland Hotel on a few occasions to network and build our brand. We toured Augusta during the Masters Tournament and opened our eyes to a whole new business strategy and partners. We were open-minded and bold.

In the spring of 2013, almost seven years ago to the day as I write this chapter, a group of women had an introductory call to start a new business. My second set of twins was about nine months old. I had three other kids aged eight and four plus a self-employed husband. It was clearly perfect timing to jump into the unknown. I believe that a person who waits for perfect timing will one day wake up and only have passed time to count, not the richness of risk and growth that business will bring. I have never wanted to watch time pass. I want to live large and face my fears, get right into the thick of things and really live out loud.

I was about to do that in ways I never could have predicted. I think that's the beauty of life, though. You don't get to know what's ahead. No amount of confidence, planning, intelligence, or even experience entitles you to a crystal ball. The truth is there is a gift in not knowing. It is terrifying if you are aware and gentle if you are not, but either way, you still don't know. No one does. Every day of early entrepreneurship is a step into the darkness with a bit of faith that the light will come. It takes a certain kind of bravery to wake up to that darkness every single day and convince yourself it is the right path. It is your calling. It is worth the risk. Most born entrepreneurs simply convince themselves it is actually the light. There is magic there. There is also a long way to fall from imagined heights.

This introductory call was pretty light and fun. Laurel and I literally "met" for the first time on that call, having been brought together by our mutual friend, Audrey, who also recruited her sister, Natalie. Cozy. Audrey's original concept was very simple: let's start an online clothing boutique. I had reservations due to some experiences in business in the past. It was nothing too negative, but I wasn't completely sure this is truly where my heart and my aspirations lay.

I'd like to repeat that: I wasn't sure this is truly where my heart and my aspirations lay. This is important. There are a million and one ways to make money in this world. I actually don't believe you have to be in love with what you are doing, but tuning in to your thoughts and the warnings your intuition is willing to send is key to success. Instead of brushing past these tiny instructional moments, embrace them. Sit with them. This was not an alarm bell. It was not a huge red flag, but I did not lean in and acknowledge that I was not, heart and soul, ever committed to the concept Audrey was presenting. Looking back, I can say with certainty that Audrey and

Natalie were. They truly loved the idea of becoming an online clothing boutique that served conservative women at an affordable price point. We each put in $5,000 and set off. It was fine.

I presented the idea that we attend a fashion trade show coming up in August and the four of us went. Laurel and I were meeting in person for the first time. This show was probably all we needed to give us that most sought after gift: a crystal ball. Again, I did not lean into the message that was being written for me. It was difficult. Audrey and Natalie had a set of values and ideals which did not jive with mine or Laurel's. Laurel and I had a defining moment in the shoe department (most women can relate, right?). We had left the others behind and set off to find shoes for our launch. We walked the aisles, studying the vendors and the options and the trends. We didn't say a lot, and we landed in a booth. We both felt comfortable and we negotiated and purchased several cases of faux leather quilted knee-high boots. Perfect. Easy. Exciting! There was one problem. Our partners absolutely did not agree. We spent too much. We didn't ask their permission. We moved too fast. Etc. Etc. Etc. Do you see the message being written for me? Still, we moved on. I was sure it was fine.

Let me cut to the chase here. We did this for another year before the business took a turn to a more specific product and we began the real work of our signature success: Pocket Innerwear. The boutique had already been selling a hot little item called a boot cuff. They were lace and had a great profit margin. Natalie had the idea after a PTO meeting one day to put a pocket in the boot cuff. What busy mom couldn't use a place to stash a card or her car keys while she is running around? We went to work and redesigned the boot cuff. This led to many more pocket concepts and, eventually, to a patented pocket. We designed. Natalie sewed and resewed. We tested, redrew, and sewed again.

Now this was true creation. Laurel began work on writing the patent, which is no small task. We got it done. We rebranded and became Pocket Innerwear. We wanted to market to everyone in the world with a cell phone. They needed us! They really did and we believed it, but it is pretty expensive to market to everyone in the world. Up to about this point, we were bootstrapping our entire business. With no debt and very little cash, we kept making it work and kept growing. We each put in another $5,000 to move the pocket concept forward.

I remember clearly, one night, I was in the back of a truck traveling from Las Vegas to home. I read an article about our own Miss Idaho who had recently won the crown. She stunned the judges and the audience when she walked on stage with an insulin pump slung on the teeny strap of her bikini bottoms. She has Type 1 Diabetes and her life depends on receiving insulin that her own pancreas no longer creates. As soon as I saw the article, I messaged the group and told them we needed to rework the pocket. It needs to work to hold an insulin pump. Now our efforts became extremely focused toward serving the Type 1 Diabetes community. We fell in love—all of us did. This was an amazing cause and a humbling venture to help people with a true need and a lifelong tiresome disease.

A couple of things happened with this shift. I found a pacing and a passion I could really get behind. I think the whole team did, too, but power struggles remained and now the nature of our goals were changing. As I ponder this time, it starts to feel more like a blur. We moved fast and connected with this community of people who really needed solutions. I loved being a part of a meaningful solution. As soon as we started putting pockets out, even before the diabetes angle, we were doing more pitching and networking in the business community. There was more to offer and explore and more reason to collaborate and find mentors.

On almost every occasion, savvy businesspeople asked a variation of the question about why we had so many partners. We were advised to simplify our structure. We were told there were too many cooks in the kitchen. The message (this one louder and more obvious) came again and again. I was stubborn and determined. At the time, I thought I was able to do what others could not. I thought I was going to overcome the challenge of these differing personalities and we would all come out on top. I truly wanted my partners to be successful. It took a long time to learn that these people were truly speaking out of love. They could see, plain as day, that the partnership dynamic would never work. They were right.

Our business morphed into a chase for retail placement. We developed relationships with Target, Walgreens, and Walmart representatives. We were now playing in larger arenas and still bootstrapping everything. We were able to do an investment round and bring in an investor who opened the sky up even more—in-house manufacturing and distribution. Laurel and I were taking the lead on these relationships and changes. Audrey had gone silent and Natalie was willing to work with us still, but I know she was uncomfortable with how things were going. She never felt valued, and I understand. Laurel and I were plowing through decisions and making relationships and getting after these retail relationships and Natalie never felt included. She also never jumped in. The resentment levels rose up slowly and built.

At the same time, we were travelling the country and taking meetings with retailers and our investor. Our investor never came through. Laurel was stacking up the debt on her credit card, and we fully believed we would catch up when we finalized things with the investor—when the money came through. There was never any money. In fact, as it turns out, there was a history of prison and run-ins with the Securities and Exchange Committee. Simultaneously, we were in bed with a manufacturer who took a partial payment to get started on a line of products for us, and it was becoming more clear by the day that he was not going to be able to deliver what he promised. It was starting to feel a lot less than fine.

I kept saying I would call it if we couldn't turn things around. I would set a date and come up to that date and find another reason to keep pushing. I don't remember the exact day, but eventually, we shut the operation down. After spending five years of my life, all those trips away from my kids, all the debt, all the mindset training, and all the people we served, it was over. It was done. I was done. For the first time in my life, I felt true defeat. It was crushing. Even as I call it back up, my heart starts to beat faster and my throat tightens, and I remember that shame and depletion. It was an ugly, dark place where I landed. My husband, my champion, my cheerleader and rock watched me struggle to get out of bed. He watched me fold inside myself and sit in silence. I was sick to my stomach and horrified at the failure. I think the word failure had become the biggest F word in my life. I feared it. I hated it. I could not accept it.

Laurel did so much better, yet she carried so much more weight. I have learned a lot from her about what true detachment means. She was able to separate this loss and keep moving forward in a way that I couldn't. Natalie was bitter and blaming and extremely difficult. She was tired and beat down, too, and held me responsible. The healing process has been so long and painful, yet it was the most incredible teacher.

The other night, I was explaining to Chad about a marketing strategy we had during the high points of Pocket Innerwear, the flaws it contained and how I will do things differently moving forward. He asked me, "So, you made a mistake and you're going to do it differently this time?" The answer I gave him really taught me that I have made it through. I said, "No, it had to be that way. It all had to be this way. I did the best I could with what I had at the time." We sat for a moment with that answer of peace and forgiveness. In that moment, I think I forgave myself for everything.

Of course, I made mistakes. Of course, there were a million better ways to do things. Of course, if I had listened to every message, I would have avoided some heartache. That was just not the way. The only way out was through. Now, instead of shame, I feel peace. Those mistakes and trials shaped me. In fact, the most awful times allow me stand here today with a breadth of experience and knowledge that comes no other way. It is not supposed to be rainbows and unicorns all the time. I can actually say I am grateful. I am grateful I was able to jump into the abyss and face the darkness and come out a bigger, wiser, more caring person. It hurt so badly. I will never lie about that. I will never sugar coat the refining process. I will respect and honor it.

I want to speak to those who are afraid. I want to grab their shoulders and look them squarely in the eyes and tell them they are right to be afraid. But they are wrong to shrink back. Go forward, even though you are afraid. You do not know what is going to happen. Therein lies your greatest blessing. Be brave! Welcome every challenge and embrace every victory! Build up your own skillset and revel in your triumphs. Fill your own cup!

You absolutely can do this. As you do it, you will become. You will become who you are meant to be. If you wait, if you let fear take over, you will only have passed time to count. The truth is EVERYONE has time. Make something of yours. Count something more significant like lives you have touched, gains you have made, and people you have served. None of those things ever went away even after I crashed and burned. They always exist and they are invaluable.

It was time to pick myself back up. I tried so many things to feel better. I do not believe there is any one right thing except forward motion. Take another step. Move until you move beyond it. What did that look like for me? I tried counseling, medication, yoga, sleeping, isolating, hiding, meditation, employment, spiritual healing. It was all forward motion. Eventually, I healed. Eventually, I stopped feeling crippling shame. I started seeing more light. I started breathing deeper breaths. I started feeling again.

I forgave myself. There is such beauty in forgiving one-self. Does anything else really matter? If you are able to forgive yourself, every other negative thing starts to fade away. The rest slips into the background and self-acceptance and flow take center stage. Try it. I want to hear from you when you do.

The timing of this opportunity to tell my story is literal perfection. Slip back in time with me for a moment. We were in the middle of our initial investment round for Pocket Innerwear. We had a really positive call with an investor who wanted in. His terms were that we simplify our partnership and eliminate everyone but Laurel and me. He only wanted to work with us. We declined. At the time, it was simple. We had another offer on the table who was willing to work with the whole group, and we were still dedicated to seeing the project through with Natalie. I wanted her to share in the success and the process. She wanted to stay, and I wanted to honor that.

As I look back, I can see a very misaligned thought process, but at the time, it felt like the right thing to do. We declined his offer and moved on with the other investor. Was I wrong? I have learned to let go of that language and label. One could definitely argue that I was wrong, but I was wrong for some noble and naïve reasons. It is so easy to look back and see the "right" way, but who would I be now? What would I have learned? What would I have given up? No matter how ugly and desperate things felt through failure and healing, I treasure the growth. I know I needed exactly what I received.

Now, in this very moment, we are reconnected with this original investor. We have come full circle and we are going back into business. A resurrection. A miracle. Funding is flowing and the flow is easy and bright. I am an open book, and I am offering an open invitation to anyone who needs help making forward motion happen in their lives. Let me help you navigate the darkness.

About the Author

Katie Larsen is a wife, mother, writer, teacher and boss lady who lives in Idaho Falls, Idaho with her husband and 5 kids. They have two sets of twins and one awesome middle child sandwiched in between. Life consists of one adventure after another and the thrill is what makes life keep moving forward. The still moments in between make it mean something.

Connect with Katie Larsen:

makingforwardmotion@gmail.com

@makingforwardmotion

CHAPTER TWELVE

Betrayals Don't Happen TO You, They Happen FOR You

By Suzanne Doyle-Ingram

I never planned to become a Mompreneur. Far from it. I also never thought I'd one day be the author of 19 books and own a book publishing company!

When my first child, Hana, was born, I thought I would find a good local daycare and go back to work right away. However, I didn't realize how much I was going to LOVE her! I suddenly had no desire to go back to my office job in the marketing department at the Korean import/export company I had been working at. Besides, when I did the math, I realized that most of my paycheck would be going to pay for daycare.

Luckily, I live in Canada, where we get 50 weeks off with pay for Maternity Leave so I had some time to think about what to do.

One day, during my year off, a friend of mine approached me with an idea. She wanted to start a business in the pet industry and asked me to join her. I thought, "Why not? What have I got to lose?" So, with no knowledge of the pet industry or publishing, we started Modern Dog Magazine.

We created a mock up of what we envisioned the magazine would look like and went door to door to pet-related businesses in Vancouver selling advertising in the magazine. Once I got over the fear of rejection, it was actually quite fun! We did really well, and that magazine is still a huge success to this day.

I worked for Modern Dog magazine for a couple of years, then moved on to a few other sales jobs in the direct marketing industry. I discovered that I loved sales. I was good at it, and I was making a great living. Life was good.

By the time we had three kids, I had started my own marketing agency. I loved it. I had several salespeople working for me and my company had revenues of over half a million dollars per year. Compared to most corporations, that is not a lot of money, but for my family, it was more than enough.

Then 2008 hit.

If you had a business in 2008-2010, you know how bad it was. When the real estate market crashed, it had a ripple effect on all areas of the economy. Suddenly, companies with whom I had signed contracts for our services could not pay their bills. Imagine having outstanding invoices for $100,000 that were never paid. All marketing budgets were frozen. It was devastating. My revenue went from $500k+ to about $80,000.

I was so stressed about money, I remember lying in bed, night after night, crying, and sick with anxiety over how I would pay the mortgage. I had a husband but felt all alone. So alone.

This went on for TWO YEARS. Two years of stress and anxiety over money. My business was limping along but I had no money for my kids' swimming lessons, dance class or anything at all.

I was down to two employees: one administrator (who I called my Right Hand Woman) and one salesperson. He became a very dear friend and when he met the man of his dreams, I helped them come to Canada to get married and I gave his husband a job.

About a year later, I had a weird feeling that something strange was going on but I couldn't really put my finger on it. One day, I Googled my employee's name and lo and behold, I discovered that he had started a company in direct competition to mine! When I confronted him, I discovered that he had gone behind my back and had taken all of our clients with him!

Overnight, I had no clients, no revenue and no clue what I was going to do. I was wiped out financially.

This betrayal took me seven years to get over. Seven years of grief, sadness, pain, and wondering where I had gone wrong. I questioned everything: Was I too nice? Too strict? Too generous, not generous enough? My mind was obsessed with wondering why he and his husband had done this to me. It consumed my every waking moment. I wondered how their business was doing... where they were getting their leads from... if they were using all the suppliers I once had... and on and on. I was consumed by it.

For a couple of years, I tried to continue with my business but it was too hard. My head wasn't in it and I felt so insecure and afraid to do anything. I somehow managed to make just enough money to cover my mortgage and my basic bills, but there was never anything left over at the end of the month. I was depressed and so very stressed.

Accepting that I had nothing left to lose, I decided to take a chance and completely pivot into a new direction. At first, I kept it to myself because I was already feeling like a failure and I had no one to talk to. I had heard about Amazon's self publishing branch and I thought maybe I could write a book.

The funny thing is, I was so insecure that I wrote it under a pen name because I thought if it totally failed, I didn't want anyone to know it was me!

The book did not fail. It actually became a best seller. And there I was, with a fake name on the book. That still makes me laugh.

Book sales were strong and I was really enjoying the steady checks coming from Amazon every month. I thought, Hey, this is fantastic, let's write some more! So I wrote 6 more books that year.

Eventually, people started asking me how to get a book on Amazon, so I put together a workshop to teach people how to write a book and get it on Amazon. Twenty people signed up for this $100 class and that's when the lightbulb went off for me. I just made $2000 teaching what comes easy to me! And I loved it! That's when my publishing company was born.

Now, eight years later, I have taught over 800 people how to write a book and I've published many of them, too. What a beautiful opportunity I have to help make people's dreams come true.

Here's what I have learned through it all

1. Never look back at the door that slammed shut because you'll miss the one that's opening in front of you.

2. Betrayals don't happen TO you; they happen FOR you. If it wasn't for my employee destroying my business, I would not be doing what I love today.

3. Keep an eye on what's trending in your industry and take advantage of new opportunities. But never put all your eggs in one basket. You can add additional revenue streams while keeping the ones you have in place.

4. Don't waste your time and energy thinking about other people's actions and behavior. Move on.

5. Always having savings in the bank. Every single time you receive money into your bank account, move a fixed amount (start with 10%) into a savings account. Start this NOW. You will thank me one day. After what I've been through, nothing gives me more peace than having savings in the bank.

If I had to do it all over again, I would reach out for help and support. I kept everything to myself because I was so ashamed of failing. Little did I know, it was happening to everyone else too! I thought I was just me.

I am so happy I took the risk and became a mompreneur all those years ago. Although there have been ups and downs and lots of difficult times (and a divorce) along the way, I have loved being able to work from home while raising my kids. We have traveled to 7 countries, and I have been able to show them things I never would have thought possible. It has all been so worth it.

About the Author

Suzanne Doyle-Ingram is the CEO of Prominence Publishing, a hybrid book publisher that allows authors to retain 100% of their rights to their books.

Suzanne is a best-selling author and co-author of 19 books. She has helped over 800 business professionals write books and get published.

Suzanne coaches and trains individuals on how to write and publish a business book, and how to use that book as leverage to increase visibility, open doors for speaking engagements, increase revenue, attract new clients and much more.

Suzanne offers FREE Book Writing training on her website at http://prominencepublishing.com/free

www.ingramcontent.com/pod-product-compliance
Lightning Source LLC
Chambersburg PA
CBHW060604200326
41521CB00007B/658